D1124541

What Is a Museum Now?

What Is a Museum Now?

and the
Snøhetta

San Francisco Museum of Modern Art

Essays by Snøhetta, Justin Davidson, and Andrew Russeth
Foreword by Rebecca Solnit

Lars Müller Publishers

Foreword

Rebecca Solnit

From any direction you can only see it partially. It hides behind the other buildings like an animal in the woods, like a face in the crowd. Although vast, it can be seen only in fragments. The buildings around it are all rectilinear: they seem static next to its biomorphic lines, which make it seem organic, alive, even feral. Viewed from various vantage points on the surrounding streets and alleys, the pale structure seems to be fluid, in motion, a little elusive for all its monumentality, like fog, like a sheet on a clothesline billowing in the wind, like a glacier gliding through the mountains.

The new San Francisco Museum of Modern Art building on Third Street between Mission and Howard (or, more narrowly, between the alleys of Minna and Natoma) is both at odds with its immediate surroundings and aligned with the deeper spirit of the place: it addresses what it means to be in a city built on change, by change, for change; a city where you constantly shift uphill or down to find new vistas appearing and disappearing, where fog blots out views, light picks out others, and then they shift; a place that has been many different places over the years, one dissolving and fading as another appears, with newcomers arriving to think it was always this way until they stay long enough to become witnesses to change themselves.

The word *gallery* originally meant spaces to walk through: placing art there to move past came later. Museums are descended in many ways from long galleries, and they are defined as much by walking as by looking. In them we roam. We pause and look at something, and we move on to look for something; we quest. Inside the building designed by Snøhetta to expand the museum's gallery space, movement becomes travel—through a landscape, through rift valleys, canyons, upward, downward, across the plains of vast galleries, across a bridge between two sections. Long staircases taper, giving an illusion of vanishing-point perspective that makes them seem even longer. The pale wood and paler walls, dressed in winter colors, remind me of California beaches, where I have walked into a sense of illimitable space.

Though lodged in the middle of a busy district, the building gives off a sense of remoteness that is uncanny. Some portions are windowless; others are lit by windows, or by doors that open onto decks and balconies. Visitors withdraw from the surrounding city and encounter it again, coming upon different vistas in different directions on different levels. A seam divides the new expansion from the original museum, designed by Mario Botta and opened in 1995. The seam allows the two buildings to move independently during an earthquake, and crossing over this seam reminds you that there are earthquakes here, like the catastrophic one of 1906 that resulted in the destruction of the surrounding neighborhood, as well as much of downtown San Francisco.

There are innumerable kinds of change to contemplate here. This very place is the result of a series of changes; more changes will come and redefine land, water, city, center, edge again. When far more of the water on this planet was locked up in ice, the coast was nearly thirty miles west of its present location, and there was neither a San Francisco Peninsula nor a San Francisco Bay. The Sierra Nevada Mountains were crowned by massive glaciers, now almost completely gone (although what comes out of San Francisco faucets is still mostly Sierra snowmelt). The now-remote Farallon Islands were hills you could reach by walking across a broad plain, and the bay was a series of valleys that funneled water into a central river, which flowed to the sea. Over time ice melted, oceans rose, the bay filled with sea- and river water, and a peninsula was defined.

The coast of the Pacific Northwest was nearly the last place on earth to be mapped by Europeans in the early modern era. From about 1650 to 1750, California was depicted (inaccurately in literal terms but accurately in spirit) as an island, separated from mainland North America by a large strait—that is, a place utterly apart. It remained a remote place in actuality until very recently, although the completion of the transcontinental railroad shaved off some inaccessibility, and air travel some more. Located at the northern tip of the San Francisco Peninsula and surrounded by water on three sides, the city of San Francisco was only converted from a place approached largely by water to one ordinarily accessed by roads with the construction of two bridges in the 1930s.

In 1847, when the peninsula was claimed by the United States in the Mexican-American War, only a few small settlements—the downtown harbor, the military Presidio, the area around Mission Dolores—dotted its vast expanse of sand and marshland. Soon after, the Gold Rush brought hordes of fortune-seekers to the area, and San Francisco became a place known all over the world. The population exploded. So many sailors jumped ship that their crewless vessels, stranded in port, were converted into warehouses and hotels. Over time the ships grew landlocked, as developers filled in the bay to create the valuable real estate of downtown. After briefly hosting a tent city, the block where SFMOMA now resides was built up early on in this transformative rush.

The spot has been many different places for many different populations. Before the Spanish arrived, the indigenous Yelamu, a subgroup of the Ohlone, had a village near its shifting sands. Today, crowds flow through the place, on their way to work or a convention, or to search out food or culture, or to return home. In between the Yelamu and the present, the area fluctuated between rich and poor, but mostly it belonged to the poor. It was a dense working-class neighborhood before the great earthquake and fire, and in the mid-twentieth century, Third Street was a Skid Row. By the 1970s it was the longtime site of light industrial manufacturing and of residential hotels full of retired waterfront workers: a poor man's world of pawnshops, taverns, diners, and cafes, of old friends and small pets. That world and almost every building in it—from Harrison to Market, Second to Fifth—was wiped away by the forces of urban renewal, which opened a path for new development and increased profits, wiped away against the objection of the old men who had participated in general strikes and waterfront politics, who fought a valiant and bloody battle against the real estate interests. Their victories are inscribed in the names of the high-rise senior residences, like Mendelsohn House and Woolf House, and in other buildings that allow the elderly and the poor to remain in the neighborhood, now dominated by affluence and transience.

A neighborhood that had served a local population was retooled as a place to accommodate changing tides of travelers and visitors from afar. With that, it lost the identity that had distinguished it from the shopping district north of Market Street (once the great divide) and instead became a part of it. Much of the neighborhood was torn down, with nearly every lot at one point or another after the redevelopment wars standing empty. SFMOMA was a latecomer, breaking ground on a long-vacant lot in 1992. The hotels Argus, Angalis, Alta, and Daton had disappeared well before, along with the Slo Boat Tavern and the Big Ben pawnshop that had once occupied the site. Nearly everything here is new, though it is one of the oldest parts of the city.

To contemplate deep time is to contemplate change and impermanence. It's to see that this precise geographical location has been many different places. It's to know that all this will change again, this place returned to the poor, or overtaken by dunes or by seawater lapping at its ruins in some age far from ours. San Francisco has changed. It is changing. It will change. The museum has been many museums over time, in three distinct buildings in two different locations over more than eight decades, and the possibilities of visual art have morphed endlessly in that time span. It's impossible to know how long the museum's future may exceed its past, or in what kind of a city the Snøhetta-designed museum may stand eight decades hence, in 2096, when the sea will have risen enough to change the coastline again, here and around the world.

Changes in orientation and perception also define a place. The Yelamu must have thought of their peninsula tip as the center of the world, but for people who drew their sense of centers and margins from Europe, San Francisco was for centuries the far edge of Western civilization, a remote outpost that was also often regarded as a refuge from the rules. That remoteness has been renegotiated over and over, but it was only when Silicon Valley exploded in recent decades to make the Bay Area a major world power that edge status ceased to define it. The history of Silicon Valley is long and exponential, reaching all the way back to railroad baron Leland Stanford's sponsorship in the 1870s and 1880s of Eadweard Muybridge's technological research, which resulted in the breakthroughs leading to cinema. (During some of that time, Muybridge lived on Howard near Third, around the corner from the current museum.) Stanford and his wife, Jane, later founded the university from which emerged Hewlett-Packard in the World War II era, and then more and more companies, venture capital firms, funds, and enterprises. Even during the dot-com boom centered in San Francisco in the late 1990s, California was still imagined as an edge, but the hugely powerful corporations that mediate, manage, and market to our increasingly online everyday lives now—Oracle, thousand-tentacled Google, Apple, Facebook—have made this region a center. They have made San Francisco, the old capital of the West in the Gold Rush era and beyond, Silicon Valley's northern border and a bedroom community from which many now commute southward to their jobs at the megacorporations. Perhaps it's apt that while the first SFMOMA building opened to the west, the Snøhetta building has multiple entrances, the grandest opening to the south.

As the center of the computing and digital information industries, a place where most of the technologies and platforms used around the world are created and controlled, Silicon Valley is a place of formidable, even world-changing influence. Like Wall Street, it is a global center of power, but it is one that undermines the very idea of centers. Information circulates fluidly across the earth and among our myriad devices, linked together by a multitude of unseen systems and networks. What seems ethereal is powered by massive server farms, placed far out of sight. Many of us during our waking hours reside in the virtual, digital realms rather than the physical and geographical, our minds wandering far from our bodies and places.

An art museum in some ways bridges the divide, as art bridges representation and presence, material and idea. Artists serve us as explorers going far into the realms of the disembodied and conceptual, dreaming of new possibilities but also calling us back to the intelligence of the senses, the philosophical possibilities of the embodied and the material, to visual and spatial perception, to the physical work of art and its aura in the age of digital reproduction. A museum exists to hold the past, to offer context and contemplative space. In this context, the building itself becomes an artwork containing all of our questions and inviting bodily travel along the miles of potential routes it offers up, past objects, images, projections, and installations; through histories, possibilities, and ideas.

Formed by Relationships

Snøhetta

In 2010 we began our search to uncover a solution to expand the San Francisco Museum of Modern Art. Together our team traveled to the city. Foremost in our search was a simple question: what is a museum? Looking for clues in the existing museum, we spent hours observing and experiencing its lobbies, galleries, and surroundings, as well as how the city and its visitors interacted with it.

It was surprising to find a level of familiarity in the way that people used the museum. Scattered throughout various corners of the building we counted some seven couples stealing kisses. It struck us that intimacy was an important part of a museum. While we understood that museums are probably not about kissing, we saw that familiarity could provide visitors with a sense of comfort in challenging surroundings. This could heighten their connection to others around them and to the art they had ostensibly come to see. This, in turn, led us to ponder a related question: at its most essential, is a museum a place for art or a place for people?

At Snøhetta we are very interested in how human beings react to, interact with, and are changed by buildings, places, and the things we make. We consider what it is that draws us into a building or, in contrast, discourages us from entering. What pulls us deeper into a space and helps us encounter change with confidence? What encourages us to linger? We are intrigued by how people form perceptions of a place. What factors influence our first impressions or inform our latent memories of having been there? The answers to these questions tell us something important about who we are as a society.

Throughout our time working on the design we spoke with a range of people including those from the museum and its benefactors, the city at large, and even a wider audience altogether unconnected to the project. We posed many questions about how they felt about the museum and how it might change. Listening engenders in us a sense of empathy for the future users of the space. This doesn't mean that we capture people's expectations or opinions and simply replicate them in three dimensions, but listening does change the way we push and pull the clay in our minds as we consider design strategies.

Concern for the interaction between humans and their physical surroundings underpins all of our work and life in the studio. Through an engaging and interactive process we believe good design can positively influence our behavior and improve our relationship with the world we inhabit. Design does this at a broad range of scales. On a societal level the work supports civic life, openness, and shared experiences as worthwhile goals. On a personal level, the designs affirm health, confidence, exploration, pleasure, and reflection. So while many of the life-affirming aspects of design are most clearly evident in public spaces, where celebrations or demonstrations typically take place, this manner of working extends beyond the collective to include the individual and the human body.

Design is a collaborative activity that relies on the individual character of each person contributing. Unlike firms that entrust a single person with the task of developing a design idea, we work as a collective, pulling together strengths from the various individual members. Everyone, from the most experienced to the youngest, brings concepts and strategies to the table. Strategies are evaluated by consensus more than hierarchy, instilling a sense of ownership in each of the many people needed to make the project a reality. This plurality of voices infuses something unique into our studio culture. While it builds richness into our work, it also ensures diverse modes of expression. There is no conscious means to stylize our buildings, and no figurehead speaks for the firm without consideration of alternative viewpoints in the group.

As the design process develops, the larger gestures and decisions are also understood on the micro level and applied to the puzzle of pragmatics. Art museums come with a unique set of problems to solve. Their contents are often extremely valuable, fragile, and sensitive to climate, and require special lighting, security, and environmental controls. Design criteria affecting the display of art can be strict, driven by curatorial considerations rather than strictly architectural ones. In addition to the needs of art there are the needs of staff and visitors to consider. Movement needs to be inviting and intuitive and should require very little signage. Under pressure to provide a variety of experiences such as eating, shopping, and educating while providing access to the art, museums face the challenge of invoking both vibrant social space and quiet places of contemplation.

This brings us back to our central question. What is a museum? Is it a place for art which happens to accommodate people? Or is it a place for people which happens to contain art? As we developed our approach to the expansion and addressed the pragmatic issues that it presented, we continued to ruminate on the museum's role, examining it from a humanist perspective at the scale of the city down to the scale of the body.

As a studio that combines architecture, landscape architecture, and other design fields within a single practice, we routinely think about buildings as part of a larger geological and biological context, even if a site is set within a city paved in asphalt. San Francisco's natural terrain exerts a palpable presence. Our feet constantly adjust to climb or descend its hills, our skin absorbs its dense fog, and our eyes delight in rapidly changing views. SFMOMA's expansion became inseparably linked to this landscape, in a way taking on the form of a landscape itself as it spread out in a broad, horizontal gesture. While studying the topography, we also looked at patterns of human settlement in the city. We traced the development of streets and alleyways that form the boundaries of the site and link it to other parts of the city. We examined the urban staircases that allow pedestrians to more easily navigate the city's steep shifts in grade. We looked at the buildings that populate the neighborhood and thought about how we might build in dialogue with them.

Somewhere between the sidewalk and the internal staircase of the new building, the city dweller becomes the museum visitor. Crossing the threshold of the building at street level and ascending to the second-floor lobby, a visitor's visual connection to the building becomes a physical connection. We look up. We move down. We see something from a distance and decide to move closer. The body leans, shifts on its axis. The world is not entirely a flat surface, seen from eye-level; bodies in motion are a component of design. Seeing and movement stimulate participation and connect us to the consequence of living. Procession in this mindset is inherently social. As you move through the building, you come upon choices: a gallery entrance on one side, a window on the other. On the stairs and landings, places to stop and rest encourage interaction and reflection. Groups come together and dissolve organically. Large windows and outdoor terraces re-immerse you in the life of the city, this time from a different perspective. The building is no longer Snøhetta's or SFMOMA's, it becomes everyone's.

In this sense, the museum feels like a place for people, dedicated to bringing us together to experience something collectively. But using the building in a direct, tangible way—sitting on it, touching it—creates a second, more intimate relationship at the scale of the body. An example of this may be found in the main stairs of the expansion, which require of each visitor a degree of physical endurance. Scaling the staircases to reach the galleries, the building no longer feels like everyone's, it feels like your own. This idea of individual ownership is important for the museum, because approaching a work of modern art can be intimidating. Often unfamiliar and challenging, this art requires energy to explore. You may be standing in front of a work with other people, some that you may know, others who are strangers. You share the space together, but also have an individual connection to the art which is entirely yours.

At SFMOMA, as in all of our work, we try to relate what is specific to a project to what seems universal to human experience. At a fundamental level, most people seek some degree of convenience and comfort in their lives. But a life led only by the familiar, the comfortable, is not a full life. Modern art's great appeal supplies proof of this. When we first approach certain works of art they shock or unsettle us. Yet discomfort often challenges our perceptions so that we might gain new perspective. Some would identify this as an essential function of all art, modern or otherwise. Architecture can function in much the same way. Buildings can challenge our perception of space and heighten our awareness of our own bodies. They can comfort us, but they can also tax us. They can selectively stimulate our senses and deprive us of stimulation, isolate us or bring us together. And like art, they can challenge the mind.

At some point while designing the SFMOMA expansion, we realized that the questions we began with could not be unequivocally answered. Or rather, by answering the questions we would sacrifice something inherently valuable in the act of asking them. A museum is many different things to many different people. Formed by relationships, between the city and the building, the building and the visitor, the visitor and the art, a museum is by nature a nebulous frame for human experience. It is a place to be together and a place to be alone together; a place to celebrate and to contemplate.

By tuning the experience of a place to the needs of its constituents, architecture has the capability of forming new and changing relationships, be they collective or individual. Although the construction of this phase in the life of the museum is finished, the city, the building, its visitors, and its art will all experience both expected and unpredictable transformations over time.

Our greatest gift as humans is our ability to interact with all kinds of things, whether they're inanimate objects or living creatures, buildings or paintings, other people or ourselves. Our work creates places that engender a valuable feeling and a memory. Ultimately, a good building is not about its particular physical qualities or visual appeal—it's about the feelings you experience while you're there and the memories that stay with you after you've left. If this is successful you will find yourself forming your own, contemporary contributions to the world you inhabit. You may find yourself refining reality.

A City Is Not a Museum, but a Museum Is a City

Approaching the museum on foot, the most familiar characteristic of the city, its hilly terrain, gradually fades from view. The neighborhood, known as South of Market or SoMa, is flatter and more familiar as cities go. The streets relate more directly to the terrain as they link nearby highways to denser working neighborhoods. Here, standing on long forgotten river beds and silty, sandy soil, the site is more about the basin than it is about the city's hills. It is a gathering place, and so too is the museum.

Nearby are the towers of the Financial District, accompanied by often partially concealed, narrow alleys. The structure of the city here is both robust and hidden and after years of neglect it has grown more polished. The alleys retain their intimacy and the museum is a part of these forgotten passages as well as the more known main streets.

Describing a dialogue with the physical limitations and conditions of the site was always a component of the design process. Slightly swooping silhouettes nestled in between towers frame the historically eccentric qualities of nearby streets. Some of the most exceptional views of the building are from alleys, offering relevance to forgotten paths in the city. One of the best ways to experience this renewed urban fabric can be found in odd locations as you approach it. Standing hard against a neighboring façade, below a fire escape, at a crosswalk or near a corner provides the best understanding of how the design works.

Inside the museum, the city continues its passageways. The atriums are an artful challenge between horizontal and vertical, light and mass, view and obstruction, gathering and solitude. The impression is that the museum and city are intrinsically connected as you progress deeper into its more contained spaces. This holds true in reverse as you leave and the dynamics form a symbiosis of connections for visitor and museum alike.

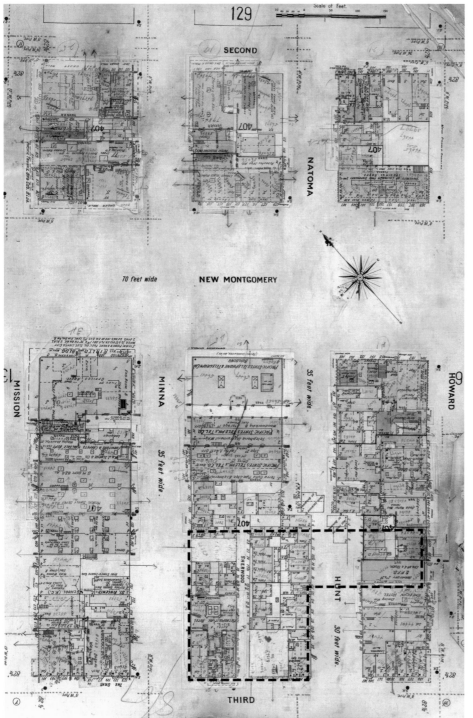

South of Market was defined for decades by dense transient populations in rooming houses and workers' hotels. Urban blight and then urban renewal turned the area into parking lots until the museum moved into the district. By the time of the museum expansion, after two decades of growth, the area's newer hotels had begun to define the district, alongside other newly formed cultural institutions.

The discontinuous city street grids overlay San Francisco's hilly terrain, which was formed by diverse geological processes. There is a strange sense of perspective: looking up at the streets from the base of a hill, the streets appear like walls. The two systems, one natural and the other man-made, refuse to yield to each other. The result has long held the attention of artists portraying the city.

much ···· Market Street
not much

St. Regis Hotel

W Hotel

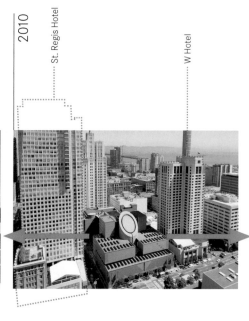

SFMOMA, which first opened in 1935 as the San Francisco Museum of Art, occupied for many years a space in the Beaux-Arts War Memorial Building, located in the city's Civic Center. This unusual home for a modern art museum was both a challenge and one of its earlier endearing qualities.

The museum moved in 1995 to its first purpose-built building. The jewel-box designed by Mario Botta announced its presence in the SoMa district and helped establish a new cultural core for San Francisco.

As museum membership and attendance increased, SFMOMA searched for ways to broaden its audience. An important mandate of the physical expansion was to open the building to the daily life of the surrounding neighborhood.

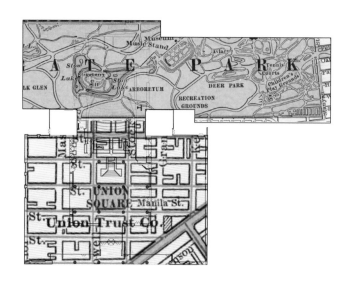

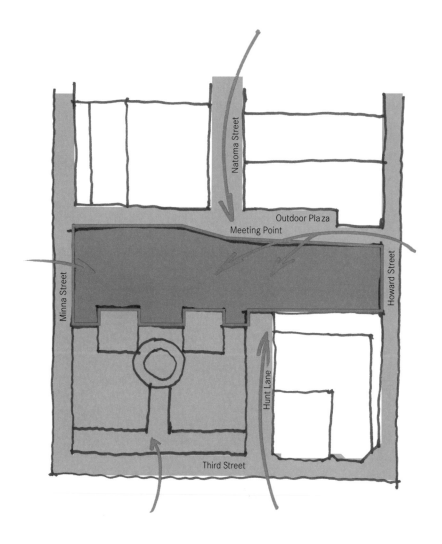

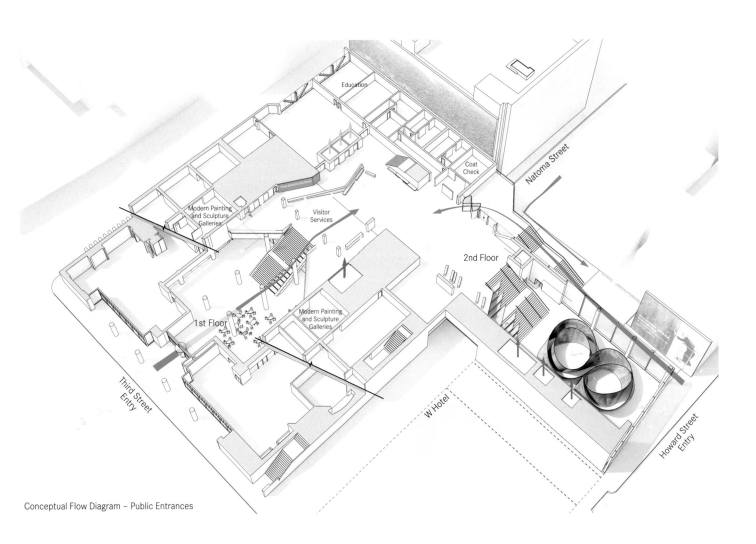

Conceptual Flow Diagram – Public Entrances

Over time the museum sought a more public face: one more accessible, transparent, and inviting to visitors. Taking advantage of a site defined by the intersection of multiple streets and alleyways, the expansion introduced multiple points of entry. Visitors now approach from all directions, attracted by views into the large interior art space on Howard Street and the outdoor art terraces above.

Once inside there is a clear sense of orientation and ease of movement. Inspired by the surrounding landscape, pathways through the building flow freely, complementing the enfilade arrangement found in the existing museum. The new configuration allows and encourages visitors to have a sense of personal choice and ownership of their experience.

A protected view corridor along the approach to the Third Street entrance informed the early sketches for the expansion project. Could the new building nestle in between its neighbors and assert its presence subtly, without overshadowing what came before?

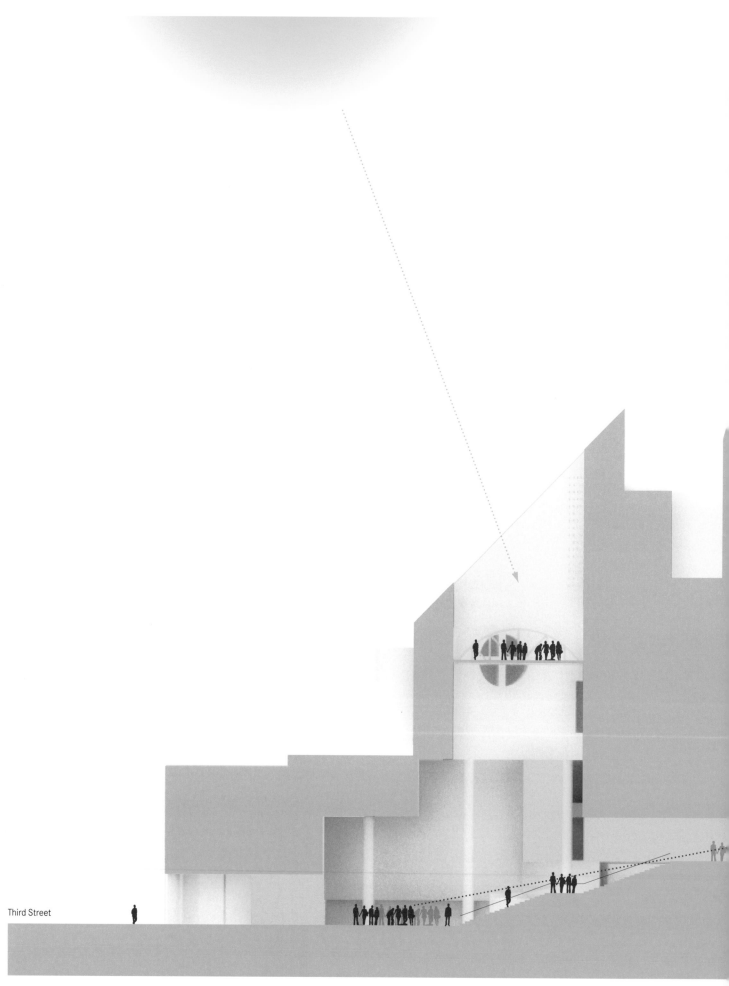

Third Street

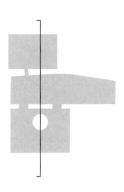

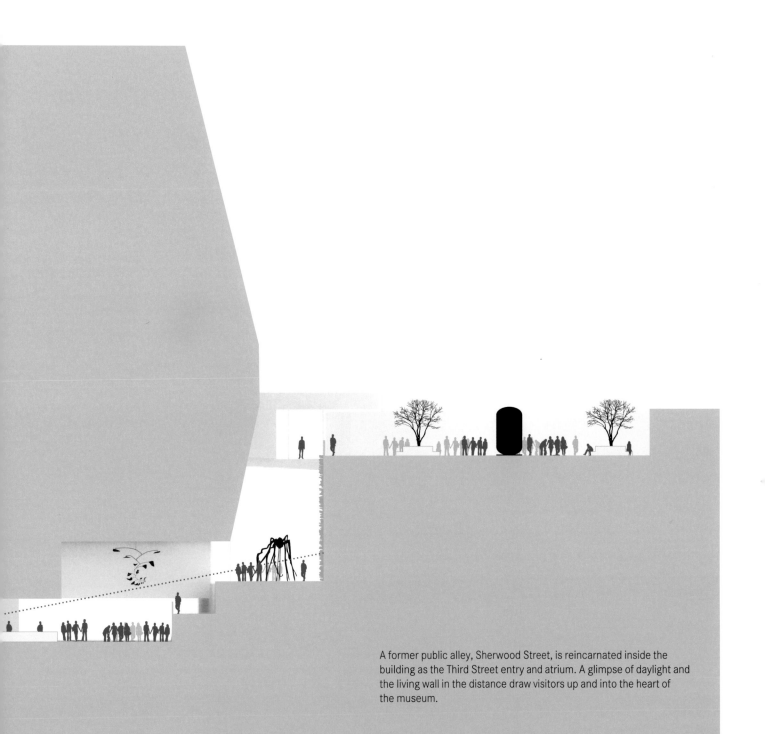

A former public alley, Sherwood Street, is reincarnated inside the building as the Third Street entry and atrium. A glimpse of daylight and the living wall in the distance draw visitors up and into the heart of the museum.

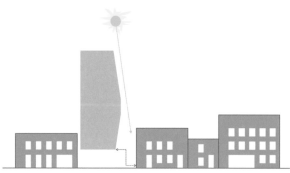

The extension's horizontal form differentiates it from a more commercial project: it does not need to maximize its bulk by pushing against the property lines. Instead the museum is released from the site boundaries, creating a new public passageway that invites visitors into the museum and its surroundings. Daylight flows down to street level from skylights and windows above, and from the spaces between the museum and its neighbors.

Hovering above a transparent ground floor, the building generously welcomes the public. The new approach places art front and center, creating an extension of the cityscape into the site and the building, and allowing the vibrancy and activity of the museum to spill out into the surrounding communities. People and art meet informally before visitors enter the body of the museum above.

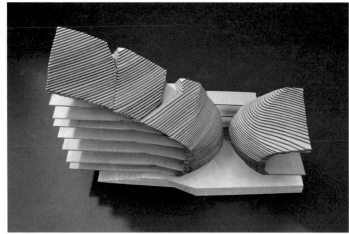

Addressing its immediate neighbors, each façade is very different. To create a strong presence for the museum within the narrow confines of Natoma Street, a variety of sculptural expressions were tested: layered, topographical, aggregate, cast, carved.

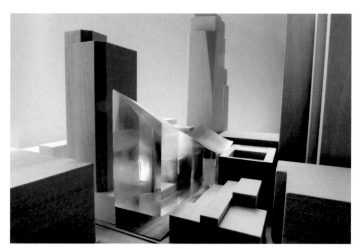

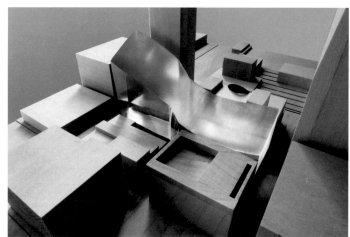

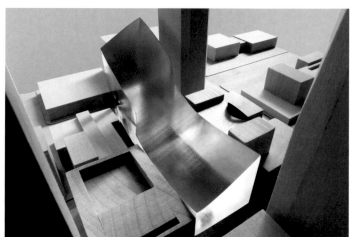

Massing studies shaped by the configuration of the site explored a predominantly horizontal form among towers. Cultural buildings, like other public buildings and religious structures, are driven by forces other than purely financial concerns. They have a direct relationship with the public and should project a distinct identity.

The designs of the street façades are different from the inner block expression. The façades on Third, Minna, and Howard Streets seem to be cut off by the power of the city, rubbed smooth by the traffic, in contrast to the Natoma Street façade, which still exists in its natural, textured state.

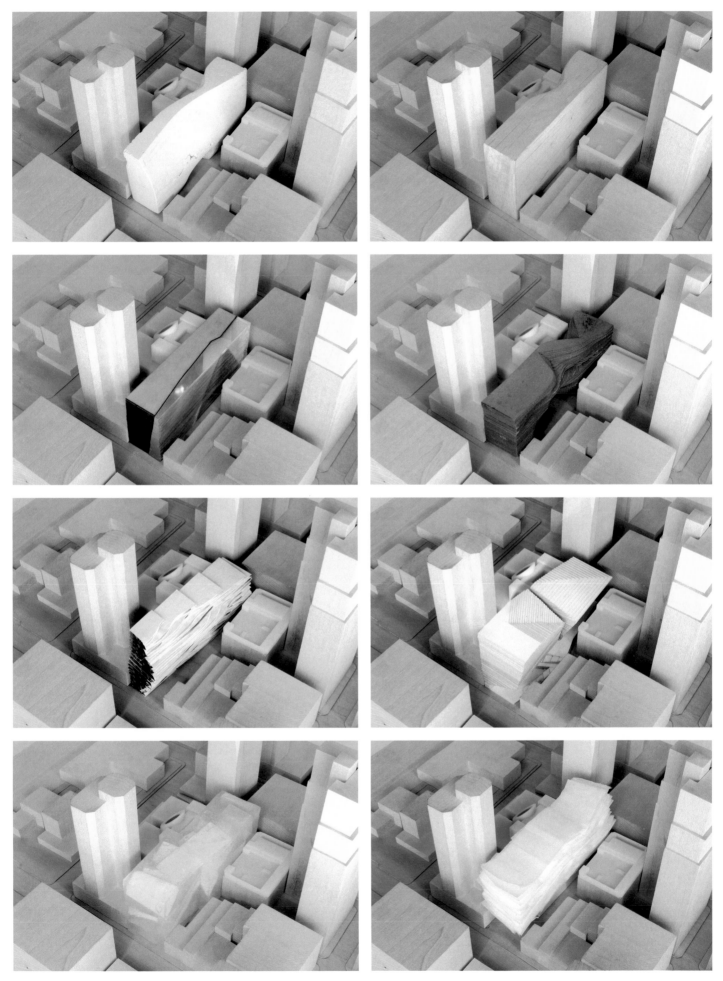

The relationship between built form and topography is more apparent in San Francisco than almost any other city.

The entry sequence builds on this relationship. The base of the building is expressed in hard, robust materials, materials of the ground. This plinth starts with the street and extends into the site. A staircase cut into the plinth lures passersby into the inner block of the museum and invites them to climb to the second floor before going inside. Along the way, views into the gallery and a glimpse of the living wall reward and encourage them.

In the center of the city block the museum can more fully reveal its form. Its curving is distinct from its more rectilinear neighbors. The form helps lead the eye into and across the site.

Getting close to the façade forms an important part of the experience. Large interruptions of the smooth form create opportunities for terraces and views. Small ripples create texture, naturally attracting visitors to the building.

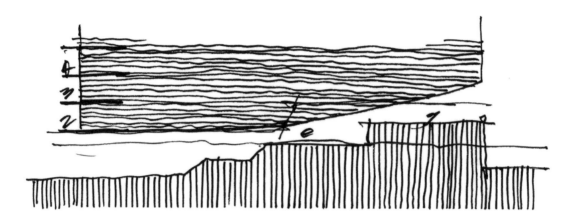

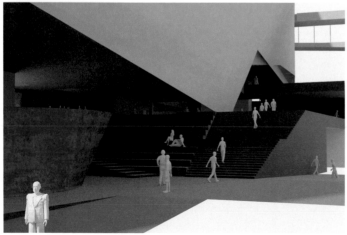

36

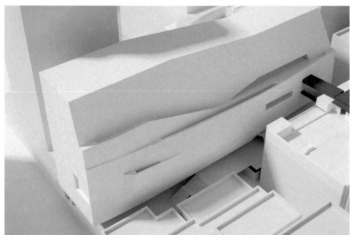
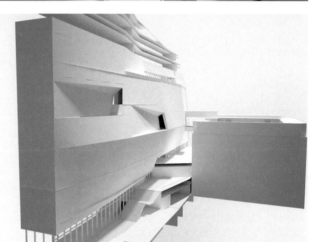
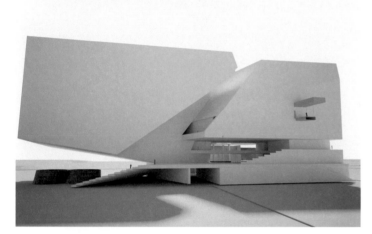
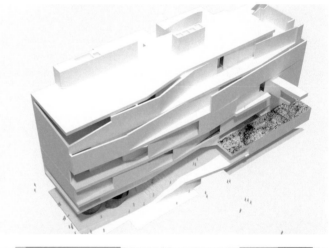
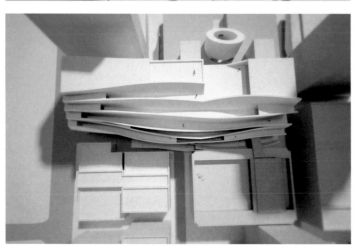
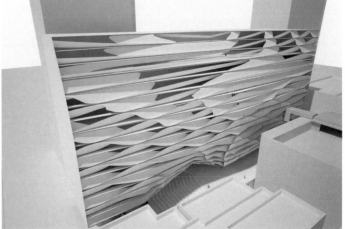

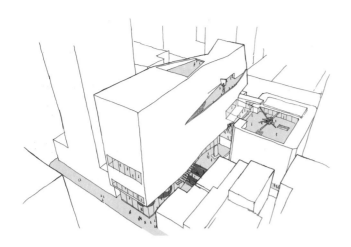

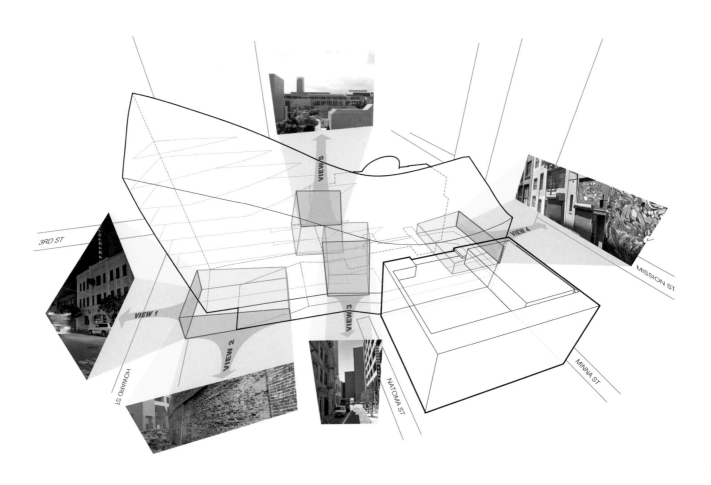

VIEW 5

VIEW 1

VIEW 2

VIEW 3

VIEW 4

3RD ST

HOWARD ST

NATOMA ST

MISSION ST

MINNA ST

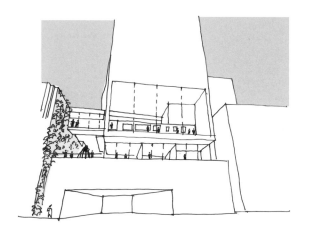

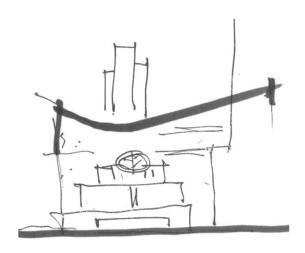

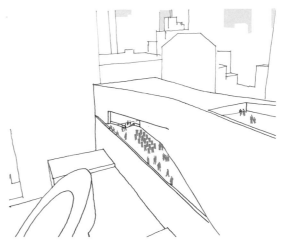

Construction Documented

Box of Contradictions

Justin Davidson

The new incarnation of the San Francisco Museum of Modern Art (SFMOMA) appears simultaneously monumental and coy. The massive extension hides its bulk in a warren of alleys, flashing glimpses of its rippled white façade to pedestrians. Walk inside and a highly controlled environment, where every light fixture and air duct has been designed to shape your experience, sets the stage for raw discovery. These oppositions—between size and intimacy, between artificiality and spontaneity—speak to the care with which the museum's architects have addressed the question *What is a museum now?*

A museum is a box full of contradictions. It is a meditative haven but also a busy arena, stitched into its neighborhood and the city beyond. A deeply democratic institution, a museum welcomes millions to view works created by rare talents. It stands apart from the market yet depends on the very collectors who drive that market. A museum enshrines the course of art and changes along with it, aspiring to be at once ageless and timely. Any architect who designs a new contemporary art museum must reconcile these paradoxes with the institution's clear, core mission: enabling visitors to make an intimate and intense connection to art.

For two decades SFMOMA inhabited a great brick and stone monument to art. In 1995 the museum moved from the War Memorial Veterans Building at the San Francisco Civic Center to a temple on Third Street designed by the Swiss eminence Mario Botta. With that commission, the museum sprang into new prominence, Botta established his presence in the United States, and postmodernism, which had dominated the 1980s, made a bid to outlive its period of popularity. The architect presented the city with a new building inspired by a composite of old ones: thick-walled Romanesque churches, terraced Mayan temples, castle keeps. His SFMOMA couches historical references in a decorative language of elaborate brickwork, contrasting tones, and patterns that run from the outside in. A wide cylinder with black-and-white sailor stripes pops out of the building's roof like a periscope, with an eye aimed at the heavens. That skylight funnels daylight down into the atrium, and the exterior stripes continue indoors as alternating bands of rough and polished granite.

Botta's handsome, block-like design was muscular enough to become an urban icon, the physical embodiment of a brand. Its symmetry ensured that it would never fade into the neighborhood that was crowding in around it. The building functions as an ornamental casket, protecting fragile artworks in deluxe galleries, behind thick brick walls. The strong design provoked strong reactions. Some critics cringed at the museum's sarcophagal appearance, but it drew audiences, donations, and loans of art, cultivating the next stage in the institution's ambitions. In the Botta years, SFMOMA answered the question *What is a museum?* by pointing to the magnetic allure of its contents: a museum is a safe, controlled viewing room for whatever its curators deem worthy. Open the doors, however narrowly, and devotees will come, because museums are known for offering a sublime experience.

The Botta building's power also defined its limitation. At a time when art was turning into a global commodity and mass phenomenon, a dynamic institution like SFMOMA could not afford to remain confined. "Many artists tell me that their work never looked better than it did in those galleries," says Neal Benezra, SFMOMA's director since 2002. "But in its strong presence, Botta's building represented an attitude toward museum design that's all about the art, rather than the visitor." He points to the opacity of the façade, which the *Chicago Tribune* critic Blair Kamin had characterized in 1995 as "surprisingly standoffish—more an intimidating fortress than an enticing people's palace."

And yet, intimidated or not, people came: attendance more than doubled almost as soon as the new building opened, and it continued to climb, topping out around 650,000 per year. By the early 2000s, both the galleries and the ballooning collection were straining at the seams. SFMOMA's success was part of a worldwide phenomenon. In those years, museum attendance everywhere exploded far beyond professionals' expectations, leaving institutions hungry for square footage. New York's Museum of Modern Art opened Yoshio Taniguchi's vast new building in 2004, which quickly became overcrowded. The Metropolitan Museum of Art pulled in a record 6.7 million visitors in fiscal year 2015-2016, after colonizing the old Whitney Museum building ten blocks away. In London, Tate Modern inflated to the size of an international airport terminal. Suddenly, running a museum required managing not only immense crowds and frighteningly swollen budgets but also complex construction projects.

Museums and cities grow together, each shaping the other. When SFMOMA chose the site for its new home in the late 1980s, it set up a frontier outpost of culture in a part of the city that its constituents considered off-limits, when they considered it at all. South of Market, or SoMa, as real estate brokers eventually branded it, spent much of the late twentieth century as an underpopulated and rundown zone of vaguely obsolescent businesses and unconventional lives. In a 2009 report, the city planning commission wrestled with the neighborhood's ambiguities: "Throughout the 1970s and early 1980s, the fate of the transitional area remained in limbo, keeping rents cheap. This factor, combined with the social and physical isolation of the area from the rest of the city, attracted populations on the margins of mainstream America, such as artists, immigrants, radicals, and gays."

Photographers, especially, were drawn to the desolation. A 1976 picture by Michael Jang shows a lone car in a vast parking lot, with the towers of the Financial District looming like a fleet of warships on the horizon. Janet Delaney spent the years from 1978 to 1986 documenting the area for a series called South of Market that paid homage to the area's tenacity: outdated businesses hanging on, derelict wooden houses hemmed in by shiny skyscrapers, immigrant families struggling to enjoy their lives in a landscape of vacant lots and half-empty warehouses. One of her pictures, *Flag Makers, Natoma at Third Street* from 1982, is exhibited in the new SFMOMA, and it shows the alley where, more than three decades later, the museum's new entrance faces the old brick warehouse, with its faded but enduring sign. Delaney also took a monumental photo of the old Mercantile Building, half a block from SFMOMA: ten stories of basic brick topped with an exuberant cornice, standing poignantly alone.

The Botta building was a monolith in this open terrain—well, almost. . . . At its shoulder rose Miller and Pflueger's 1925 Pacific Telephone & Telegraph Company Building, sheathed in white terra-cotta and bejeweled with sculpted eagles. Soon, the work of urban reclamation—demolishing low-rise warehouses and parking lots to make way for glass towers—got under way. As SFMOMA's board contemplated a new expansion and bought up adjoining property, it was faced with a set of contradictory demands: how to outgrow and at the same time preserve Botta's assertive showpiece; how to respectfully integrate the original into a bigger, busier museum; and, above all, how to grow into a neighborhood that the museum had helped transform.

Today, SFMOMA is a juggernaut crouching in a forest of high-rises. The forgotten lanes, like Natoma, Minna, Tehama, and Clementina streets, are less neglected now, memories of the industrial past mingling with intimations of wine bars yet to come. The sign above Henry's Hunan, on Natoma, still bears the carved words "N Clark & Sons," reminding passersby that the address once served as the office of a long-defunct brickmaking operation. Miller and Pflueger's telephone building now houses Yelp, as well as the high-end restaurants Mourad and Trou Normand. In the surrounding streets, a new cultural district has taken shape: it includes the Yerba Buena Center for the Arts, the Museum of the African Diaspora , the Contemporary Jewish Museum, and the future Mexican Museum. Once the new Transbay Transit Center opens a couple of blocks south, thousands more pedestrians will stream out of the station and flow along Natoma Street toward SFMOMA.

Those future crowds will see not an ostentatious monument but an enigmatic slice of architecture levitating at the end of the street. Everything seems off-kilter: the dark space that turns the lane into an apparent dead end; the stair ramp that crosses at a rakish angle; the crinkly façade scored with a vertical slash of window, asymmetrically placed; the building that bulges, waves, and rears back as it moves up toward the sky.

To get a complete view, I head to the roof-deck of a nearby condo. Only from above can you fully appreciate how ingeniously Snøhetta's architects managed to maneuver a generous building into a tight and narrow midblock lot. It vaults over a neighboring hotel's loading dock and presents one narrow end to the main artery of Howard Street, all while adamantly refusing to disappear. From this elevated vantage point it appears to be rising out of the spume, a soft and wrinkled creature, caught in the interval before it snaps into bland, right-angled conformity with its block-mates. This is a structure that disrupts and harmonizes at the same time.

In the same way that a new coat of paint in one room can make the other rooms look suddenly shabby, a new architectural presence exerts a powerful, and not always flattering, influence on its immediate surroundings. John King, the astute architecture critic of the *San Francisco Chronicle*, writes of the expansion, "Think of the mountainous cultural complex as a giant lens that magnifies everything around it on the block.... Buildings with character come into sharper focus. Sloppy details turn bleak. Life on the ground is amplified for better or worse."

Los Angeles Times critic Christopher Hawthorne scanned a slightly wider horizon in his review of the building, musing on the expansion's role in the city's fast-paced development. He describes the cultural building as "practically tripping over itself to stand down and out of the way" compared with the new commercial buildings, "blithely taking up as much space in the sky as they can." To Hawthorne, this "seems typical of the balance of power in the new, money-drenched San Francisco." Craig Dykers, one of Snøhetta's founding partners, bridles at the idea that the new SFMOMA aims to be deferential. "Commercial buildings are almost always built out to the property line and then go straight up, as far as they can. Ours is horizontal, and it doesn't touch the property lines at all. It's a signal that commerce is not the city's only driver."

Like all good architects, Dykers appreciates constraints. Snøhetta has produced its share of freestanding monuments, like the Norwegian National Opera and Ballet in Oslo, the National September 11 Memorial Museum Pavilion in New York, and the Bibliotheca Alexandrina in Egypt. (The firm has also designed smaller solitary objects, such as a pavilion for viewing wild reindeer in the Norwegian mountains.) But a solo structure comes with its own kind of burden. It's the architectural equivalent of an operatic tenor walking onstage with a follow spot: he gets to shine, but he'd better deliver. SFMOMA, by contrast, takes its place in a contrapuntal ensemble of buildings, many of them bigger, taller, and more assertive.

From up on the neighboring roof-deck, I can feel the museum's architecture negotiating between rigor and flexibility, between the rectilinear street grid and the mercurial art within, between plasticity and permanence. The façade contributes to the illusion that the physical museum is a living thing. From a distance the quarter-inch-thick membrane looks fluid, but in fact it is stiff, stretched over the bellying shape. Handmade, tough, and moody, the cladding continually adapts to the city's ever-shifting weather, going soft in the fog or glittering against the acid-blue sky. As with ornament-encrusted buildings like Miller and Pflueger's of a century ago, the shadows flatten out as the sun arcs high, then deepen toward evening, the façade acting as a kind of sculptural sundial.

It's tempting to see the surface, and the form behind it, as the product of a digitally besotted age, the dernier cri in mass customization and software-aided eccentricity. It's true that the building springs from its technological moment, a time when designers and suppliers can collaborate to develop, mock up, test, manufacture, and install new products in new configurations, all with computerized predictability. But in this case, the result bears such vivid traces of other human hands that it makes me want to reach out and touch it.

Today virtually all architects depend on computers to aid in design. Various software programs help them develop multiple iterations of an idea and generate immersive images of still-imaginary interior spaces. At Snøhetta, digital tools take their place alongside pencil and paper, plaster of paris, saws, sanders, and dexterous fingers. The model shop—located in the center of the studio and surrounded by glazed conference rooms and rows of monitor-bedecked drafting desks—contains plenty of hand and power tools to slow down the iterative design process. Through physical experimentation, project team-members explore and exchange formal, spatial, and material ideas and evaluate alternatives. Designs percolate, moving between physical expression and digital representation until consensus solidifies. This process led, in the case of SFMOMA, to the creation of countless digital schemes and more than one hundred physical models, ranging in size from very small to full-scale: sixty of these models now reside in the museum's collection.

In the museum project, the idea for ripples or striations on the building façade came early, an outgrowth of contemplating the site's proximity to the Pacific and active plate tectonics, which produced its distinctive geomorphology. Experimentation with various types of model materials—wood, clay, and paper among them—led to diverse expressions of this idea. "One model we made for SFMOMA," Dykers explains, "is small—the size of your hand. We made it by creating a little paper form and then pouring concrete into it. . . . Then when we pulled the formwork off, we saw it . . . created strange lines on the model, and although we had been thinking about lines on the façade, it wasn't until we saw all those incidental ripples that we understood what we were looking for." The team simultaneously investigated similar effects through digital modeling, the one influencing the other. This led to new explorations and discoveries—and eventually, the distinctive striations of the new SFMOMA façade.

Fabricating the exterior cladding also required mixing new techniques with traditional craftsmanship. Snøhetta supplied the California-based company Kreysler & Associates with digital instructions for forming 710 individual panels, each one with its own particular topography. Kreysler's computer-controlled milling machines carved each shape out of foam. Workers used these to create molds that were then filled with liquid fiber-reinforced polymer (FRP) and allowed to harden. The surface of each resulting panel was finished by hand with old-fashioned sandpaper. The result looks delicate, even liquid. But actually, a tester who subjected the shell to a sledgehammer attack left only a tiny abrasion: if I needed to keep the weather out of a research station at the North Pole, this is the stuff I'd choose.

Back at ground level, I walk along Howard Street and pause at an expansive glass wall where Richard Serra's *Sequence,* a 213-ton assemblage of rusting steel walls, curls in on itself like some industrial-age Stonehenge. Along that see-through gallery, a new pedestrian alleyway leads to an outdoor staircase and entrance. The approach feels almost surreptitious: I sidle up to the strange creature of a building and slip through the glass doors. Inside, the atmosphere is festive. Visitors wander in and wind their way into the center of Serra's labyrinthine sculpture*,* idle on the stepped platform, or gather beneath Sol LeWitt's huge, exuberant *Wall Drawing 895: Loopy Doopy (blue and white)* in the second-floor lobby. If the exterior crooks a finger and winks at passersby, the public areas reassure them that they've come to the right place.

I ask Benezra whether this laid-back come-on to the curious, followed by a friendly, art-filled starting point, was meant to project a new vibe. The director nods but points out that a policy of encouraging people to come for pleasure rather than to fulfill their cultural duty has a venerable pedigree by now. "Museums' attitudes toward the public started to change with the Centre Pompidou in Paris, which opened to the public in 1977," Benezra says. "It evolved of a populist idea that art is not just a precious thing" for connoisseurs, but a resource for everyone, and that "a museum is a place where people gravitate. It's open until 10 p.m., you can come in for free, there's a big plaza out front, and people go there for a lot of different reasons. It took a while for that idea to take hold, but when we wrote our strategic plan, we really wanted SFMOMA to be a great place for art, but an equally great place for people."

With that populist program in mind, the board turned to a firm that didn't have a long catalogue of museums under its belt, but one that had resoundingly proven it had absorbed—and advanced—the lessons of the Centre Pompidou in another sphere. In 2007 Snøhetta completed the Oslo Opera House, which wraps the city's social life around a dockside auditorium. The roof doubles as an elevated piazza, which inclines along its sides and down toward the fjord. This is a cultural center you can walk around, through, and over—and people do. Benezra hoped their new expansion would translate the democratic spirit they sought into equally concrete form. "It was risky for us to commission a design from a firm that didn't have an extensive museum background, but it actually proved to be of great benefit, because they were open to looking, and thinking, with us," he says. "They didn't come with a signature style that they were going to impose on us: they listened."

In San Francisco, Snøhetta's architects didn't have the Oslo project's spacious site, or its spectacular waterfront location. Instead they amplified small gestures, made Botta's art fortress more permeable, and sowed the extension with welcoming details. That's why the journey through the new museum is dotted with moments of respite, like the wide window seats in the hallways outside many of the galleries that provide glimpses of the world outside. On the third floor, the architects pulled the building back from its neighbor, opening up a space just big enough for a long and narrow sculpture terrace flanked by a great green wall. That vertical garden is at once cool and spectacular, an invigorating brush with nature. It contains more than nineteen thousand plants in thirty-seven different species, all watered by recycling storm water, gray water, and condensation from the museum's air conditioning system.

What I admire most about the new SFMOMA is that these detours and pauses don't distract from the art but rather prepare the mind to be receptive. I don't need a museum design to lure me inside, but I appreciate being coaxed into staying. "Having a live connection with greenery is relaxing," says Lara Kaufman, one of Snøhetta's project architects for SFMOMA. "It has a direct physical effect on your experience in the museum. In school they teach you that architecture is about the whole body and that what you see affects how you feel. We talk about this a lot as we design." In an institution governed by the maxim *Don't Touch*, Snøhetta has created a sensual, tactile experience. "When you touch the wooden handrails they have a super-silky feel," Dykers says. "The light maple floorboards are installed to 'float' above the building slab, so they quiet your footfall and cushion your step as you walk through the gallery spaces."

That concern for physical comfort, combined with a tangle of code issues and the desire to fuse old and new, prompted one controversial trade-off: the decision to remove Mario Botta's staircase from the Third Street atrium. Those who remember SFMOMA in the pre-Snøhetta days recall the staircase as a totemic sculpture, a kind of vertical mini-temple entered through a vaguely ominous portal striped in matte and polished stone. The stairs seemed designed mostly for descending: they fell in two parallel cataracts past white, shelf-like balconies, then joined at a narrow opening and spurted out onto the ground floor. Handsome and dramatic, they served mostly to suggest that new arrivals might want to take the elevator up instead. Virtually everyone did.

Expanding the building triggered a new safety requirement: with its greater capacity for visitors, the museum required more ample stairs, to avoid bottlenecks in case of an evacuation. Widening Botta's staircase to meet building code would have meant moving the columns that hold up the roof and effectively rebuilding the atrium. Instead, the architects replaced the staircase with something more practical. Benezra explains, "We wanted to be respectful of the [Botta] façade, certainly, but at the same time, the building has got to work."

Not everyone was convinced. Hawthorne called the decision to honor the original building and at the same time scrap its most distinctive interior component "odd," leading him to question, "Should the museum simply have knocked down the older building and started from scratch on a prominent and roomy site?" Dykers concedes that if you narrow your focus to architectural aesthetics, starting from scratch would have been the purer option; but that was never on the table. Dykers continues, "That stair was memorable, and memory is a good thing, but does that make it valuable enough?" Similar questions haunt virtually every block of every evolving city, including San Francisco, and the answer is always different. Here, I find myself torn, recalling a lovably impractical original yet recognizing that the price of saving it might have been too high.

Snøhetta replaced Botta's four-story vertical unit with a wide, asymmetrical climb that winds up through the atrium, hiding the steepness of its ascent to the second floor. The new staircase connects the original building to the new, the street-level atrium to the lobby on the second floor, and the Third Street entrance to the new one on Howard Street. The vocabulary is pure Snøhetta: gray terrazzo steps, long maple boards in a pale blond finish, polished wooden handrails, glass railings. It's as if the new part of the building were reaching down into the old, beckoning visitors to the upper levels, where most of the art is on view.

Above the second floor, another set of stairs becomes a vein running up through the building's inner cavity, with the upper flights tightening like canyon walls. An indoor hiker, I pause at balconies and view both the path I've taken and the segment still to climb. For Snøhetta, staircases designed in the spirit of adventure resonate with the extreme contours of San Francisco: the climbs to Telegraph Hill and along Filbert Street, the sumptuously tiled Sixteenth Avenue steps, and the plunging pathway down to the Sutro Baths out at the city's western edge. The galleries lead viewers on a horizontal itinerary of the imagination, from one artist's fantasy to another; the stairs turn the transition from floor to floor into a more physical kind of passage.

As I pass from the public spaces to the hallways on the fourth, fifth, and sixth floors, their wide windows facing toward the Bay Bridge, I can feel myself drawn into the museum's core: three central floors of galleries, lovingly designed to disappear. Since a museum's most essential task is to hang art so the public can see it, these crucial spaces are designed to be the building's most self-effacing. It's easy to get galleries wrong, erring on the side of airless or echoey, dim or glaring. Ceilings can be too high or too low; the walls inflexible; the proportions off. Just think of every time you packed into a crowded corner to view a masterpiece hung by an ill-placed doorway, or noticed a sculpture that seemed lost in a hangar-like expanse. Curators need maximum flexibility, but achieving this is an art in itself.

Soon after Snøhetta won the job, they joined a small group of SFMOMA staff and board members on a museum tour of Europe and the United States. "Those visits raised Snøhetta's ambitions: they said, 'We want to build you the most beautiful galleries of any museum in the world,'" says Deputy Director of Curatorial Affairs Ruth Berson. "It was a process of getting there without making a loud architectural statement in the galleries, while at the same time minimizing the appearance of everything functional." The architects understood that all of the gallery's guts and moving parts—air returns, grates, wires, outlets, access panels, and fire sprinklers—needed to disappear. So, too, did the points where temporary walls can be fixed to the ceiling to reconfigure the galleries for different exhibitions. To achieve that outrageous simplicity, the architects fitted out the ceiling with undulating series of coves containing cable channels and ambient light fixtures. Outside, the exterior walls ripple erratically; in here, a uniform wave rolls soothingly across the ceiling.

Many curators abhor natural light, which can wreak havoc on delicate artwork. Accordingly, the architects placed windows out of alignment with gallery entrances so that daylight has to sneak around corners. In each room the gentle radiance of the outdoors mixes with the ambient glow of hidden LEDs, which matches the sunlight's direction and intensity. Perhaps no visitor would notice if the ceiling coves emitted the wrong tone of light in the wrong direction, but Dykers insists that getting the illumination right can affect the artistic experience in subliminal ways. "Your body can *feel* light, just like it feels sound," he says.

The new SFMOMA offers an abundance of answers to the question *What is a museum?* The building's meanings shift and evolve and rub against each other depending upon who's standing where at what time of day. To the city planner the museum is a magnetic hub, increasing foot traffic and transit demand. The real estate broker sees it as a value-boosting neighborhood amenity. The neighborhood office worker on a lunch break values it for an hour's pleasant refuge. For the passionate art lover, it is a sanctuary, a school, a second home. Snøhetta's design honors all these disparate uses and definitions, gently pointing its users to the simple ritual of gazing at one object, then another, and another.

In religious buildings, we often sense the motion toward increasingly sacramental spaces: a marble threshold before the nave, a step up to the bimah, a screen marking off the chancel. In most museums, on the other hand, visitors barely notice the equivalent transitions, as they duck from a hallway into a gallery while hunting for a restroom or cafe. At SFMOMA, though, I register the purposeful passage from the urban world outside to the artistic one within, from bustle to contemplation. I leave behind the busiest elements—slashing stairs, startling views, unsettling undulations—just as I shrug off the most tangled parts of my day, and arrive at a sequence of serenely unprepossessing chambers.

"There's always a need for introspection in a museum," says Kaufman. "As we penetrate deep into the building, we have to be able to refine our thoughts. Galleries are made for those moments of reflection. They are not transition spaces; they are self-contained, inward-looking."

And yet a gallery is far from an anodyne cell. Rather, it's a soothingly neutral place that nurtures emotional extremes. We come to these quiet enclosures to experience the wildness of exuberance or terror. This is where artists like Anselm Kiefer are free to fill the blank walls with bursts of complicated anguish. Entering into an intimate relationship with works of power can be uplifting, revolting, even dangerous. But as I step toward them, I am grateful to the architects for ensuring that I am primed and ready, my limbs loose, my mind clear. *That*'s what a museum is for.

What Is a Museum without People?

Museums are both places for art with people in them and places for people with art in them. They are also, at times, neither of these things. Most importantly, museums satisfy a need to form connections both surprising and familiar. It is about not simply looking "at" art in a museum, but becoming embodied within it for a moment in time.

To create an authentic bond with a place and a collection, it is important that the building's design goes beyond satisfying its basic functional demands. It should be formed around the full range of human behavior and the senses of those people using it. Design in this context cannot rely solely on dialectic or metaphysics. Architecture helps to refine reality, bring corners into view, sharpen perception and dialogue. It can make the invisible visible, better supporting thought while approaching complex works of art.

San Francisco's maritime climate envelops the city in its ever-changing phenomena of light, fog, water, and salt. The city's vernacular architecture of white and pastel crenellations register the bright sun and clouds passing over its undulating streets. The new museum façade speaks a similar language, one of constant animation and movement. It is a dialect of tactility as well, one that invites passersby to draw close and touch its unusual skin.

Crossing a horizontal entry threshold, a vertical challenge is introduced as the galleries climb seven stories upward. The physicality of climbing up or down changes your perspective and behavior. Stairs require physicality: heart rates rise, blood flows a little faster, the brain fills with oxygen. The effort needed to move vertically reminds us that we are alive. Stairs and slopes are also places for engagement. Negotiating up and down creates unexpected situations. Pairs might split into single file. Passing strangers brush shoulders, making sudden eye contact in the shared challenge.

Even if a visitor is not able to use the stairs, there are similar sensations when arriving on different floors in the building; the city drops away, albeit never far. Window seats naturally gather people together and frame distinct views onto the city and into the museum. Outdoor terraces near gallery spaces provide direct contact with the elements, sunlight and fresh air. Here, the building reconnects to the experience of the city and its landscape, to the invisible things, and to the many desires of those that come to it.

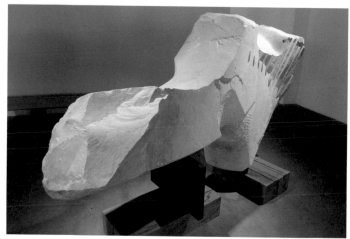

From the ground looking up, buildings sometimes loom large, like the sheer face of a cliff. To compensate for this challenge, details can bring buildings into a more direct relationship with the human body.

The exterior expression of the SFMOMA expansion creates a symbiosis of scale, linking the immensity of geologic patterns to the middle scale of the urban and the human scale of the visitor.

Isamu Noguchi's sculptures, where traces of natural forces comingle with marks of the hand, produce a similar effect.

Public staircases help pedestrians navigate San Francisco's extreme topography, resulting in one of the city's most iconic experiences. Walking along a street, views dramatically unfold and abruptly close. The city comes close for a moment before disappearing. Even the weather joins the game as the fog bank rolls into the city and frames first a building, then a bridge.

Some of these staircases form ceremonial passageways through the city. Others feel highly social, like an extension of the porch or the driveway. A few, cut into hillsides overgrown with vegetation, create verdant escapes.

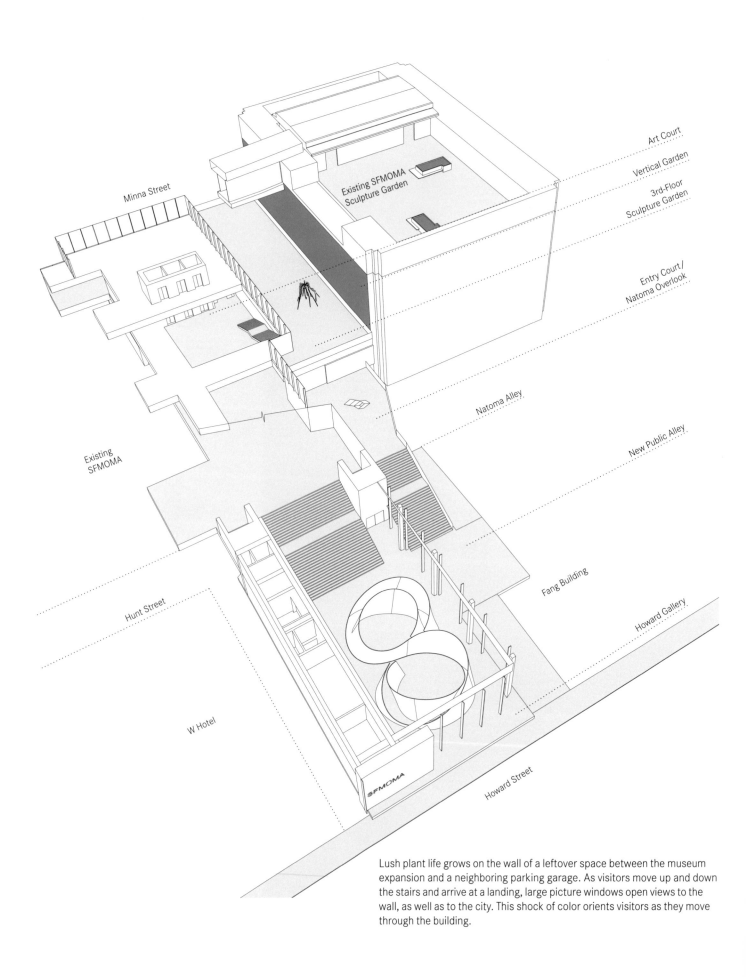

Art Court

Vertical Garden

3rd-Floor
Sculpture Garden

Existing SFMOMA
Sculpture Garden

Minna Street

Entry Court /
Natoma Overlook

Natoma Alley

New Public Alley

Existing
SFMOMA

Fang Building

Hunt Street

Howard Gallery

W Hotel

SFMOMA

Howard Street

Lush plant life grows on the wall of a leftover space between the museum expansion and a neighboring parking garage. As visitors move up and down the stairs and arrive at a landing, large picture windows open views to the wall, as well as to the city. This shock of color orients visitors as they move through the building.

Minna Street

Howard Street

Single-Floor Museum

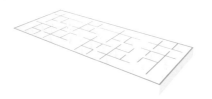

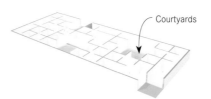
Courtyards

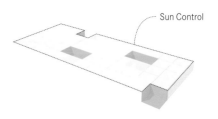
Sun Control

Vertical Museum

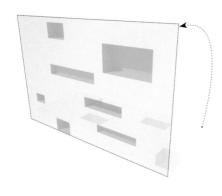

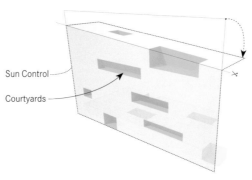
Sun Control
Courtyards

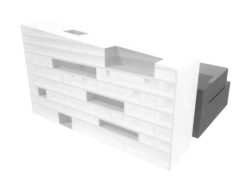

Open Space Diagram

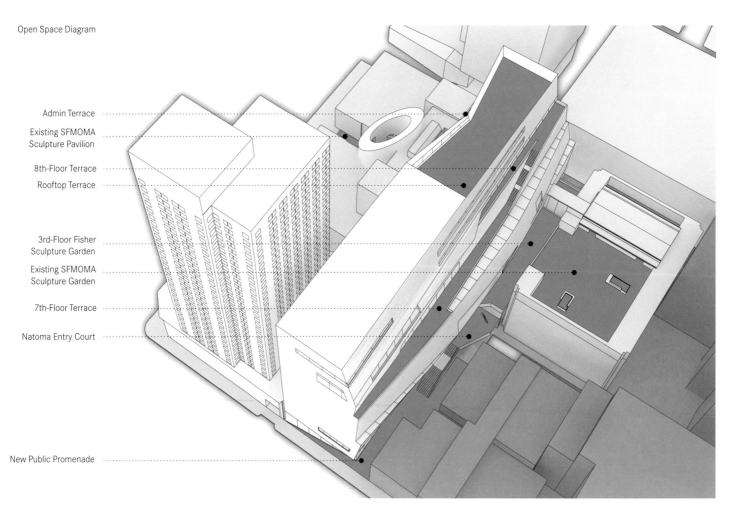

Admin Terrace

Existing SFMOMA
Sculpture Pavilion

8th-Floor Terrace
Rooftop Terrace

3rd-Floor Fisher
Sculpture Garden

Existing SFMOMA
Sculpture Garden

7th-Floor Terrace

Natoma Entry Court

New Public Promenade

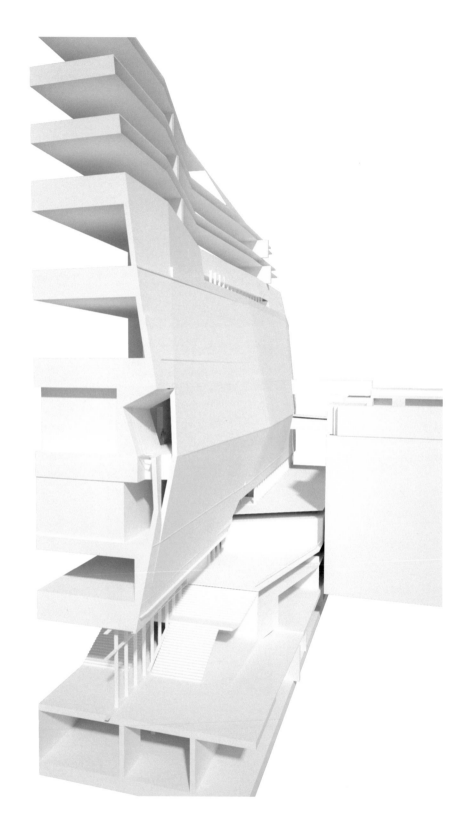

Outdoor terraces connect the museum back to the street and to an
alternative art experience. The stairs, landings, and terraces bring
San Francisco's public staircases and alleyways into and up through
the museum.

Somewhere between the sidewalk and the interior staircases of the building, the city dweller becomes the museum's visitor as visual connections become physical. Numerous paths lead visitors up into the museum to begin exploring the collections. In addition to the main staircase, there are other unique stairs, as well as elevators. Some of the stairs are very delicate and rather small. Others are grand and monumental. One is even hidden.

The stair system connects all the galleries to each other and to the outside. The vertical spaces of the staircases funnel and curve to distort traditional rules of perspective. Climbing the stairs creates a heightened sense of drama and anticipation around entering the galleries and viewing the art.

The main stair is intertwined with the building façade: on the top four floors, as the stairs weave up and down they fit into a narrow zone slotted in between the core galleries and the undulating façade. This edge is neither city nor gallery; it is something in between. At their highest point, the stairs lead to an outdoor terrace. Outside, visitors come close to the skin of the building, touching its surface directly.

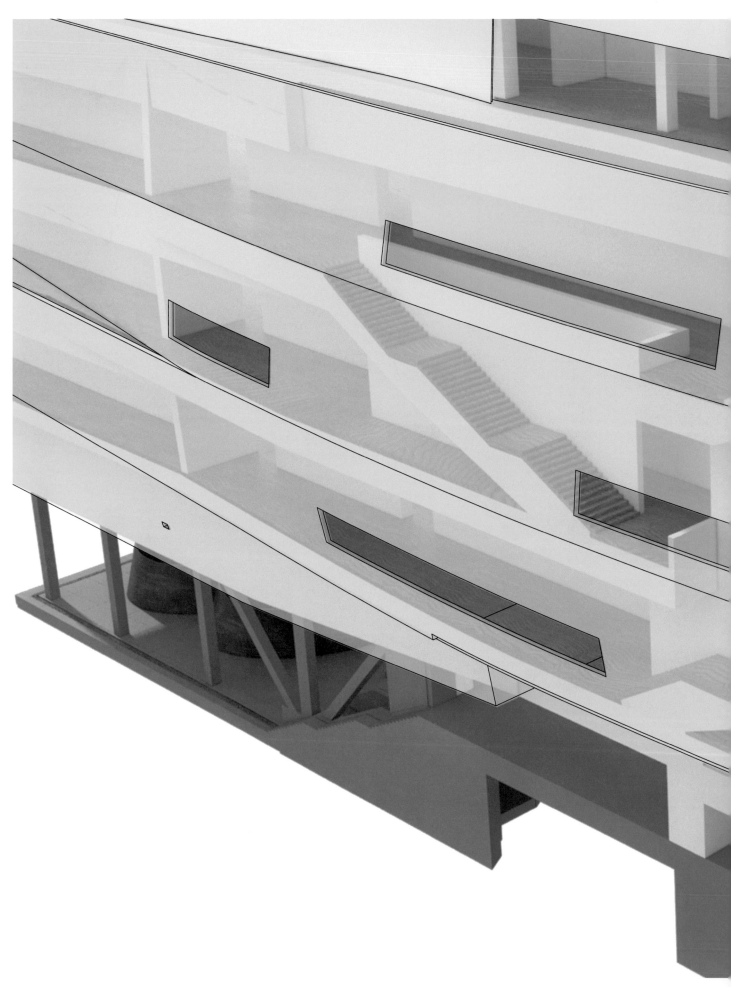

The sculpted horizontal form generates changing patterns of light, attracting visitors from a distance, through the eye, and up close, through the hand.

The fiber-reinforced polymer panels formed in fluid ridges accentuate the play of light and shadow across the surface and react to changing conditions. The panels have areas of exposed reflective aggregate to pick up and reflect sunlight. They provide a human scale as people approach.

Numerous drawings, models, and mock-ups were made at various
scales over the course of many months to refine the façade expression
and performance.

Technical analysis of the geometry and curvature of the façade panels helped the ideas develop into buildable components. Full-scale mock-ups confirmed the project's aesthetic and performance expectations.

The rippled façade geometry is made of fiber-reinforced polymer (FRP). FRP is incredibly durable and lightweight, which helped reduce the weight of the building. This reduced weight improved the structural design of the building, allowing for lighter and smaller structural steel than would have been necessary with a concrete, stone, or masonry façade.

The 710 FRP panels are each unique and required custom tooling to produce. The fabricators found ways to do this economically: since all of the tooling only had to last a single use, it was possible to make the molds out of EPS foam, which is very inexpensive, lightweight, machinable, and recyclable. A side benefit of the custom tooling is that once the panels were cast, the molds served as perfect-fitting custom handling cradles for every panel. The curved FRP panels are attached to unitized aluminum curtainwall panels which are planar, insulated, and standardized into a limited number of families for efficiency at the weather seal.

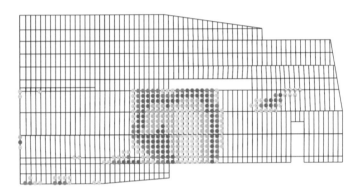

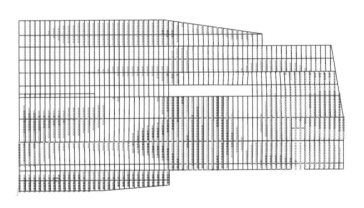

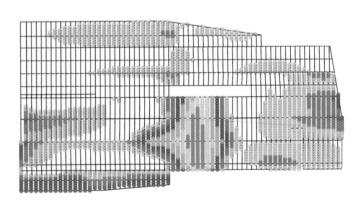

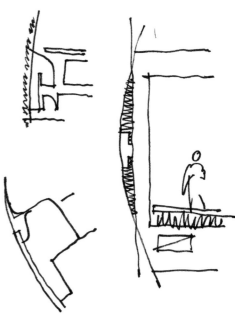

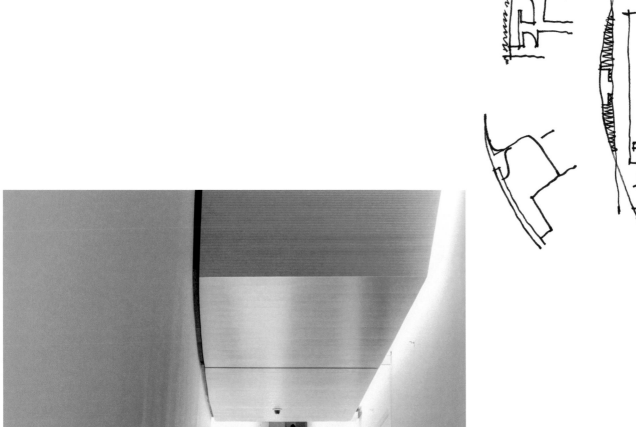

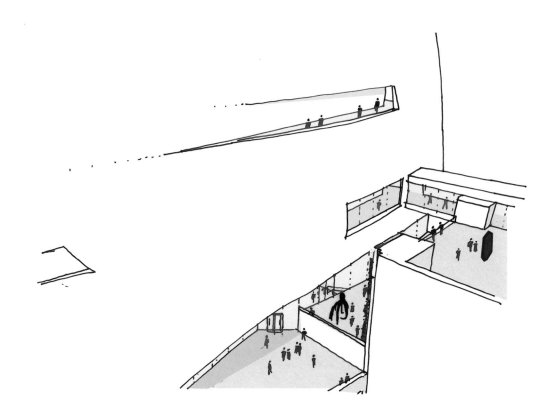

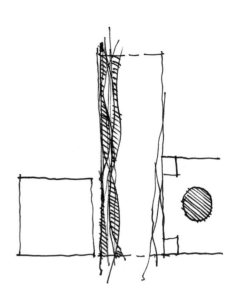

SFMOMA Facts

235,700 ft.² (21,900 m²)	Usable square footage (USF), new expansion building
225,000 ft.² (20,900 m²)	USF, original building (after renovation)
137,000 ft.² (12,730 m²)	USF, total gallery space
45,000 ft.² (4,180 m²)	Free public access areas in the expansion
84,389 ft.² (7,840 m²)	Rippled façade system area, comprised of 710 unique fiber-reinforced polymer (FRP) panels
	SFMOMA is the largest building to use the FRP façade system in the US to date
4,400 ft.² (409 m²)	Living wall planted area, composed of 21 different native plant species, 17 non-native plant species, and 19,442 individual plants
255 ft. (78 m)	Length of core galleries
55 ft. 8.5 in. (17 m)	Longest steel span
25 ft. (7.6 m)	Longest cantilever, Level 6
7 ft. 6 in. (2.3 m)	Deepest girder, Level 7
500 ft. (152.4 m)	Speed per minute of new public elevators
19 tons	Weight of new atrium stair steel structure
22,051 tons	Weight of new expansion building (above Level 1)
47,758 tons	Weight of new expansion building (below Level 1)
14,657 tons	Weight of original building (above Level 1)
28,850 tons	Weight of original building (below Level 1)

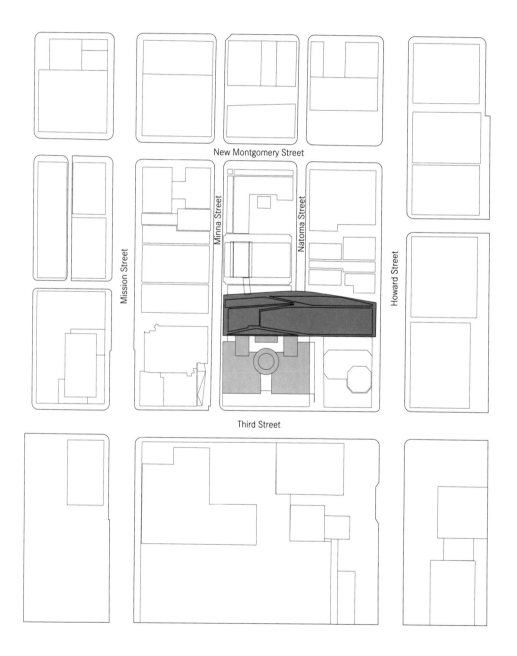

New Montgomery Street

Mission Street

Minna Street

Natoma Street

Howard Street

Third Street

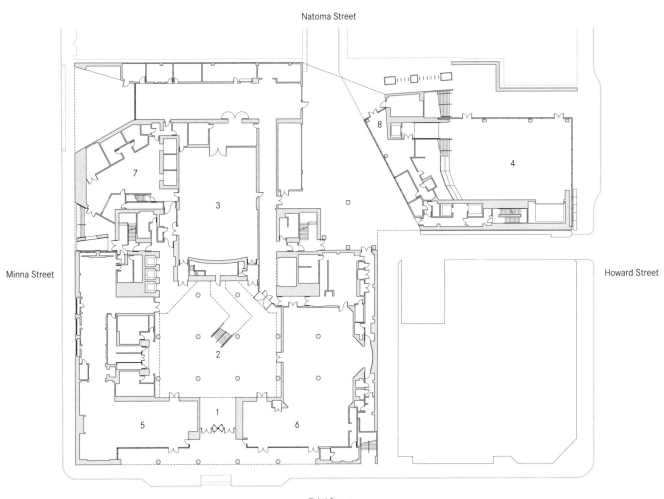

Natoma Street

Minna Street

Howard Street

Third Street

Floor 1

0 10 20   40'

1 Entrance at Third Street
2 Atrium
3 Theater
4 Gallery at Howard Street
5 Museum Store
6 Restaurant
7 Entrance at Minna Street
8 Staff Entrance at Natoma Street

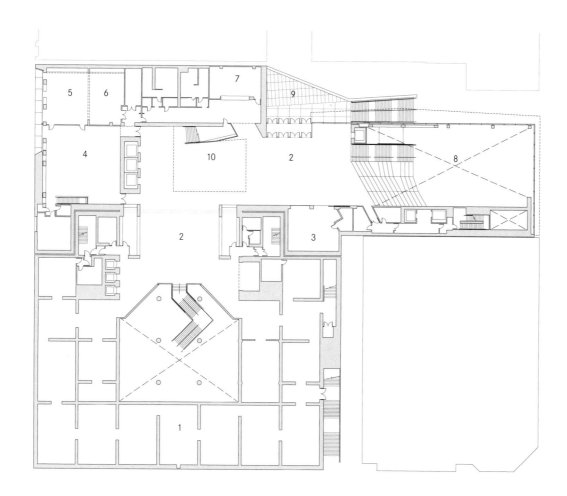

Level 2

1   Painting and Sculpture Galleries
2   Lobby
3   Museum Store
4   Education Center
5   Studio 1
6   Studio 2
7   Coat Check
8   Gallery at Howard Street
9   Entrance from Howard Street
10 Art Hall

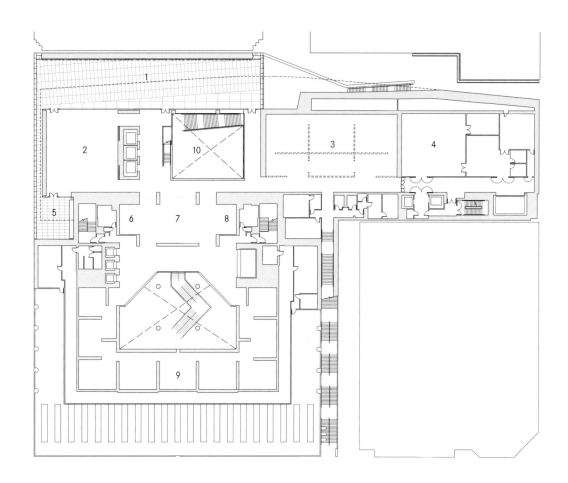

Level 3

0   10   20   40'

1 Sculpture Terrace and Living Wall
2 Calder Gallery
3 Photography Galleries
4 Collections Study Center
5 West Sculpture Terrace
6 Gallery
7 Photography Interpretive Gallery
8 Coffee Bar
9 Photography Galleries
10 Art Hall

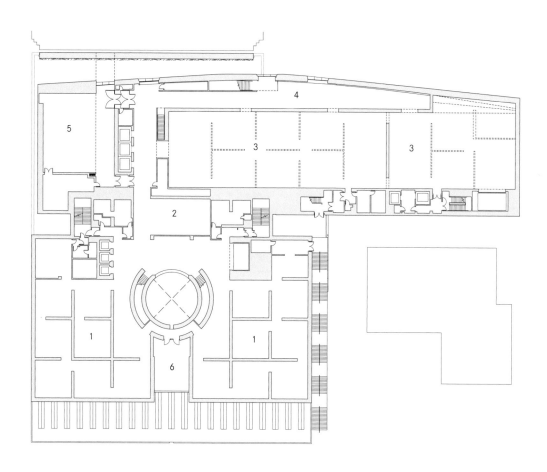

Level 4

0   10   20   40'

1 Special Exhibition Galleries
2 New Work Gallery
3 New Painting and Sculpture Galleries
4 City Gallery
5 White Box
6 Sculpture Terrace

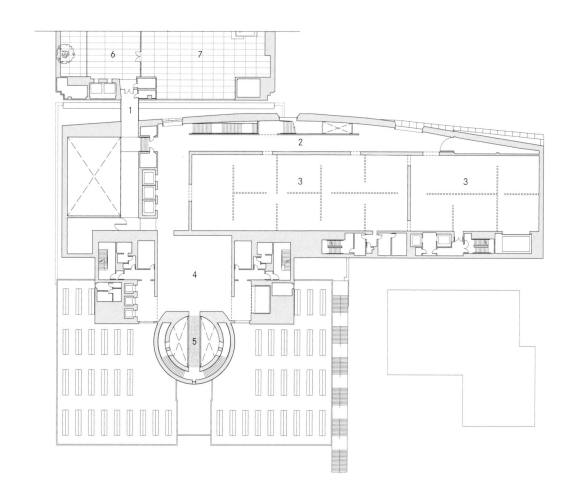

Level 5

1 Bridge
2 City Gallery
3 New Painting and Sculpture Galleries
4 Sculpture Gallery
5 Oculus Bridge
6 Cafe
7 Sculpture Garden

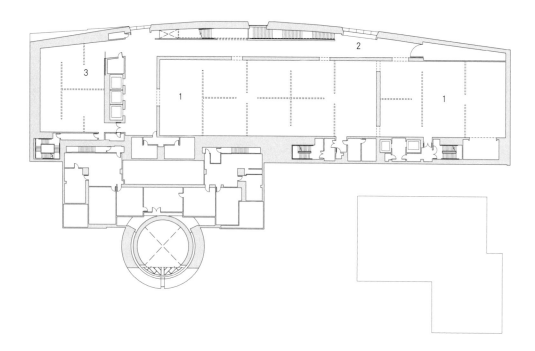

Level 6

0 10 20   40'

1 New Painting and Sculpture Galleries
2 City Gallery
3 Architecture and Design Galleries

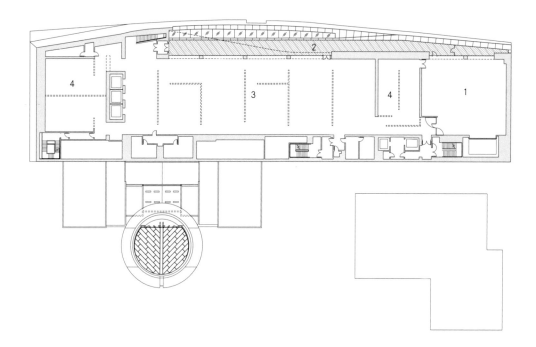

Level 7

1 Conservation Studio
2 Sculpture Terrace
3 Contemporary Galleries
4 Media Arts Galleries

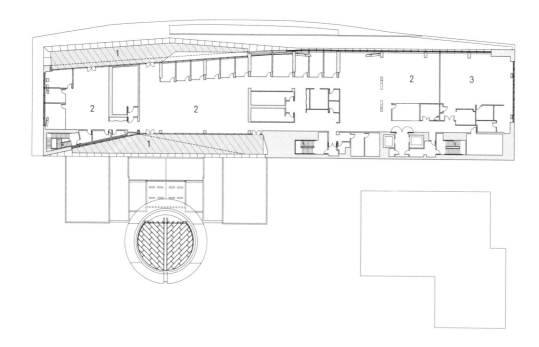

Level 8

0   10   20   40'

1 Terrace
2 Administrative Offices
3 Conservation Studio

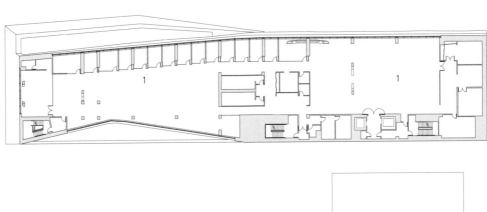

Level 9

0 10 20   40'

1 Administrative Offices

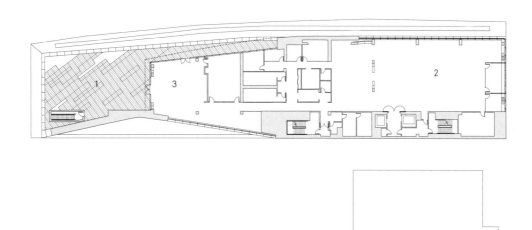

Level 10

0   10   20   40'   ⊕

1   Terrace
2   Administrative Offices
3   Pantry

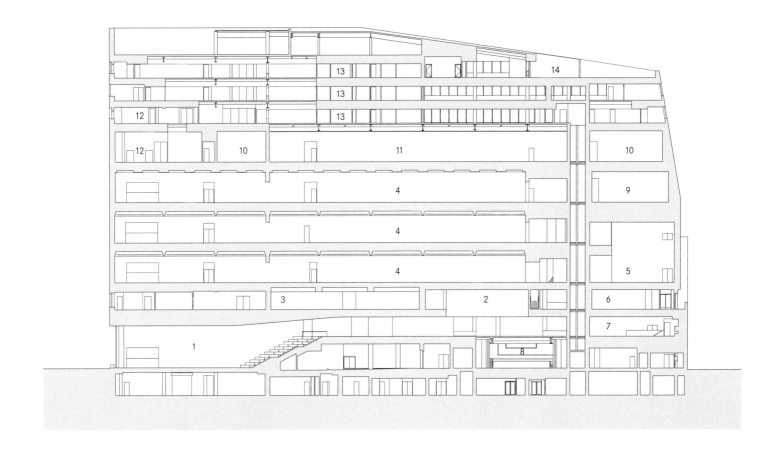

North-South

0   10   20   40'

1 Gallery at Howard Street
2 Art Hall
3 Photography Galleries
4 New Painting and Sculpture Galleries
5 White Box
6 Calder Gallery
7 Education Center
8 Theater
9 Architecture and Design Galleries
10 Media Arts Galleries
11 Contemporary Painting and Sculpture Galleries
12 Conservation Studio
13 Administrative Offices
14 Terrace

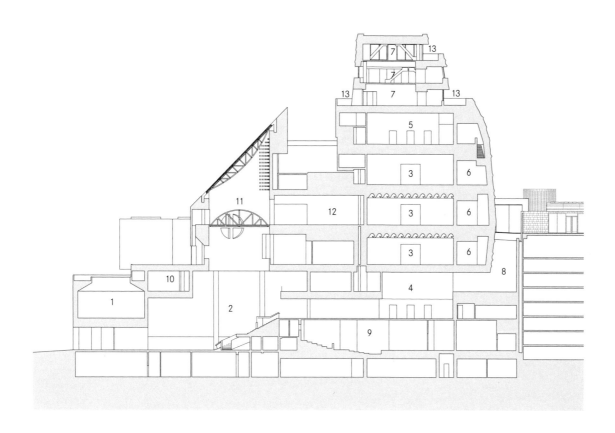

East-West

1 Painting and Sculpture Galleries
2 Atrium
3 New Painting and Sculpture Galleries
4 Art Hall
5 Contemporary Painting and Sculpture Galleries
6 City Gallery
7 Administrative Offices
8 Sculpture Terrace and Living Wall
9 Theater
10 Photography Galleries
11 Oculus Bridge
12 Sculpture Gallery
13 Terrace

Coming into Sight

Andrew Russeth

In 1970, the Bay Area artist Tom Marioni invited friends to meet up at the Oakland Museum one evening and have a few drinks. He intended the party as an art action and titled it *The Act of Drinking Beer with Friends Is the Highest Form of Art*. A few years later, he began staging the event weekly, serving beer because "it's the American sacramental wine."[1] It is an undeniably goofy conceit, but it is also a quietly profound one, highlighting various transfigurations: what happens when people come together, when quotidian activities become art, and, of course, when sobriety turns toward inebriation. Marioni cordially invites his guests to pay attention—to the world, to each other, and to themselves.

This risks sounding fanciful, but *The Act of Drinking* has always struck me as a solid little analogy for today's art museums, crystalizing their interlocking and sometimes competing missions. They serve as places for reflection, yes, but also for conviviality and for heady, maybe even life-altering, experiences. They must fulfill manifold obligations and welcome diverse constituencies, becoming constellations for aesthetic revelations and social gatherings, theater and music, business and play. Balancing those responsibilities is not an easy task. It is a management problem with architecture at its center, as the museum building sets priorities and delimits possibilities.

Those are not the only lines that art museums must straddle. Around the time that the Museum of Modern Art opened in New York in 1929, Gertrude Stein is said to have quipped, "A museum can either be a museum or it can be modern, but it cannot be both,"[2] making a point that Theodor Adorno would deliver even more explicitly in 1953 when he wrote, "Museum and mausoleum are connected by more than phonetic association. Museums are like the family sepulchers of works of art."[3] Art museums, but especially art museums dedicated to modern and contemporary art, are today tasked with accomplishing seemingly contradictory goals, preserving culture while at the same time embracing contemporaneity, making a space that can render both art of the past and art of the present moment with acuity. The mausoleum must be made to feel utterly alive.

Which brings us to the newly expanded San Francisco Museum of Modern Art, a structure that handily manages these numerous tasks, elegantly offering up new ideas about how museums can function and interact with the communities they serve while at the same time creating opportunities for a multitude of experiences.

Even from a far distance, one can see that something fresh is afoot at SFMOMA. Walking toward it through Yerba Buena Gardens one sees the expansion, a silvery white, rippled curtain of a building, hovering behind the imposing brick structure, conceived by Mario Botta, that opened as the museum's first purpose-built home in 1995. Reading the new building from the street is a tricky business. Made of more than 700 unique, computer-modeled, fiber-reinforced polymer panels, the façade shimmers ever so slightly, thanks to sand from Monterey, California, that has been embedded into the material. Craig Dykers, a founding partner at Snøhetta, has likened it to the fog that hovers so low in San Francisco, drifting in from the sea, and the waves that churn on the waterfront.[4]

Like the rolling landscape of the city, and like so many of the works inside the museum, the building's façade is elusive, always shifting into something else.[5] As in Ruth Asawa's beguiling hanging sculptures of the 1950s, which she made by weaving metal wire, minute decisions are working together to create captivating, sui generis curves.[6] The façade's mystique also recalls Robert Irwin's work of the 1960s and 1970s, when he was pushing art into realms of phenomenological enigma, painting minute dots on panels so that a piece's color is unclear, or working with Plexiglas discs and light so that its borders are unresolvable, seeming to stretch into the wall. Such moments of uncertainty are signs of serious and unusual aesthetic experiences, as words slip away before something new. "To see is to forget the name of the thing one sees," as the poet Paul Valéry once put it.[7]

Is it possible for art museums to encourage their visitors to see better, to be somehow more alive and alert to the artworks they contain and to the world that surrounds them? The notion, proposed by Snøhetta, seems at first mention to be far-fetched. But many of us have had those memorable moments—perhaps getting lost in the black depths of a Lee Bontecou construction from the 1960s or peering through the semi-translucent skeins of animal fiber that cover pairs of shoes embedded in walls in Doris Salcedo's *Atrabiliarios*.[8] Your eyes are shocked. Your mind shifts.

Similarly intriguing things occur at the expanded SFMOMA. Entering through the old entrance, off of Third Street, into Botta's soaring atrium, one finds a new intensity to the sun streaming through the oculus. Its armor-like stairs have been removed, freeing up the view from floor to sky. The angular new staircase, paneled in wood—probably the most controversial aspect of Snøhetta's design—sets you ever so slightly off balance, the first of many elements that playfully wake you up.

Just as SFMOMA now presents itself to the surrounding city in various ways, eschewing a single, frontal profile, it also offers various entryways to its guests. In addition to Third Street, one can come in off of Howard Street, walking through a post-industrial square along a tall gallery. Walled with huge sheets of glass, this space is a luminous sign to the public that they can come in and wander through the Richard Serra sculpture *Sequence* (2006), which will reside there for the next few years. Stepped seating at the back of the gallery, leading up to the new lobby, extends an invitation to linger. If the original Botta entrance aimed to awe visitors with the grand power of open space, Snøhetta's Howard Street counterpart strives to seduce passersby inside, to entice them to meet up and relax. The threshold of the museum becomes permeable. This happens again on a shaded sculpture terrace, three floors up, where one catches glimpses of the city around a soaring vertical garden.

Around a bend from the Howard Street staircase is a third path leading to the museum. Staff can enter through a door protected by a porte cochere there, and visitors can wind around to the new entrance. This approach to the museum is the one that thrills. It runs down sleepy Natoma Street—more of an alleyway really—lined with offices, a parking garage, and windows of shops and restaurants (formidable hunks of meat can sometimes be seen mid-preparation). Walking along it offers up the strange sensation of sneaking up on this hulking, diaphanous building. A new city transit hub is under construction a few blocks away, and once it is completed, it will be fascinating to see if this tranquil stretch is transformed into a more traditional thoroughfare, with businesses shifting their orientation to address new throngs, or whether some of its private, subversive character will remain intact.

A building helping its visitors see, welcoming them in multiple ways, becoming almost transparent at points, and presenting changing visages to the city—these features of Snøhetta's expansion, and others that I will address later, signal a sea change in the history both of SFMOMA and of art museums in general. They denote the formation of an emerging typology, though fully recognizing it requires jumping backward in time a bit.

SFMOMA's founding was similar to many of its peer institutions, in both an architectural and an institutional sense. Local patricians established it in 1935 as the San Francisco Museum of Art, placing a pioneering director at its helm, the curator Grace Louise McCann Morley, then in her mid-thirties. It first opened on an upper floor of an existing building, the stately 1920s Beaux-Arts War Memorial Veterans Building, like so many art museums before it (the Louvre palace, for example, which became a public gallery in post-revolution Paris in 1793). But quite unlike many of the museums that opened around the same time, the San Francisco Museum of Art (it became the Museum of Modern Art in 1975) remained in its original home for nearly sixty years, from 1935 to 1994. During that long stretch, many of its compatriots forged ahead in constructing architecturally au courant buildings—Frank Lloyd Wright's Solomon R. Guggenheim Museum in New York in 1960 and Lina Bo Bardi's São Paulo Museum of Art in 1968, to name just two examples from a lengthy list. And many of these museums expanded, some repeatedly, with increasingly grand gestures, aiming to reach a broader audience and show new forms of art. All the while, SFMOMA remained in its thoroughly traditional setting.

Odd though it is to write this, the restrooms are where Snøhetta most overtly presents its aims for the new building, its desire to intensify the process of seeing. They are painted, floor to ceiling, in single, intense tones, a different color on each floor. It is most dramatic on the second floor: a potent red fills the room—and the eye. People enter, smile, laugh, even scream. Almost invariably, they snap photos. Exiting the restroom to the sight of white walls, one's vision is immediately cloaked in green. It takes a moment to realize that an afterimage has taken hold. Seeing is thus foregrounded as an activity that is fragile and dependent, always under the influence of other factors, whether of the mind or of the world. The rooms are palette cleansers or tonics for vision: they remind us to think through our most basic experiences. How do we know what we see? How do we know that we are seeing the same things that others see? What is real, even? Fairly impressive questions for a bathroom to spark.

You are also made aware of your own sight at other, decidedly subtler, moments, which creep up on you slowly. A few come in the long hallways—the city galleries, as they have been informally termed—that run along the side of the Doris and Donald Fisher Collection, the new main exhibition spaces on the fourth, fifth, and sixth floors. These loggias ease transitions from stairwells that run alongside the building to the galleries. Sunlight streams through ample, angled bay windows that seem to riff on the now-iconic trapezoidal ones that Marcel Breuer installed in his 1966 building for the Whitney Museum of American Art in New York, with the added bonus that these feature comfortable wooden window seats—perfect little rest stops, delivering varied views of the vertiginous city. They allow you to look out, as far as you can see, right before you do the reverse, confronting an artwork up close.

The wall that runs against the building façade is curved slightly in two directions, which allows visitors to sense the connection between the interior and exterior. These hallways were intended as slightly more informal galleries, and the displays of art are likely to be fairly spare at most times, allowing the eyes a respite, preparing them for more art-filled galleries. During SFMOMA's inaugural post-expansion installation, works by Isamu Noguchi and Joel Shapiro looked wonderfully at home, with plenty of room for them to breathe.

These pathways narrow as they go up through the building, which is an almost invisible means of orienting the viewer—a device more likely to be felt than seen—and the curved wall arcs overhead, altering the character of the sounds during the walk. Meanwhile, interior windows in the city galleries provide views of stairwells on other levels, an M. C. Escher-like presentation of the circulatory structure, hinting at what is to come.[9]

The stairs also challenge visitors a bit. Conceiving them, Snøhetta looked for inspiration at some of San Francisco's lengthy urban stairwells.[10] While those at SFMOMA are, thankfully, not quite as long, they can leave even the reasonably fit climber a touch winded.[11] As visitors catch their breath on a landing, they look down the hallways of the building, considering where to head next. The jagged, quick-cutting stairs of Zaha Hadid's 2003 Contemporary Arts Center in Cincinnati provide a precedent for the stairs at SFMOMA, but while Hadid's shoot through the building at slightly odd angles, providing unexpected glimpses of the galleries, Snøhetta's steadily climb the building, with a view onto the city always visible. Ascending them becomes a kind of journey.

These stairs confer on us the role of the *flâneur*, wandering the city, taking it all in. We stroll this vertical environment, dodging the occasional person, our heads darting up and down and out onto the cityscape. Baudelaire said that the *flâneur*, on the hunt for "the poetic in the historic," strives to distinguish "the eternal from the transitory."[12] Is this not exactly what we do when we look at art, finding in objects of the past what can move us here in the present?

The total SFMOMA project stands in sharp opposition to what Hal Foster has described as a brand of contemporary architecture that "tends to subdue us, for the more it opts for special effects, the less it engages us as active viewers," where "'seeing oneself see' approaches its opposite: a space (an installation, a building) that seems to do the perceiving for us."[13] This, Foster argues, tends to happen when architects take phenomenological interests off the deep end, making "environments that confuse the actual with the virtual."[14] Both inside and outside, in marked contrast, SFMOMA engages us—it treats our perception and our experiences as things that are worthy of care and consideration, by shaping space and light and volume through subtle means.

The timing of SFMOMA's architectural developments is interesting to consider in this regard. The Botta building arrived in 1995, right before the turn toward spectacle and hypertrophy in art-museum design truly crescendoed. Frank Gehry's sprawling Guggenheim Bilbao would open in 1997, with its "blimp hangar spaces"—as Robert Morris would characterize them—where "even dinosaurs would get lost,"[15] followed in 2000 by Herzog & de Meuron's Tate Modern, with its cavernous Turbine Hall and its large-scale corporate commissions. Twenty years after Bilbao, Snøhetta's SFMOMA provides evidence that this mode of museum-making is slowly petering out, at least in some quarters.

One reason for this shift, I suspect, is a natural backlash to the art world's single-minded fixation on big-budget entertainment and a renewed interest in collections and traditional artworks, as well as the architecture that serves them. Changes in economics and taste have also played their parts. Morris muses that Gehry's Bilbao "allegorizes the spirit of the gigantic multinational corporation,"[16] but the capital most likely to be accreted in the form of a museum now is that of private individuals or families, who prefer discreet displays of wealth (relatively speaking): David Chipperfield's 2013 Museo Jumex in Mexico City and OMA's recent Fondazione Prada in Milan and Garage Museum in Moscow (both on repurposed sites) come to mind.[17]

Mercifully, markers of commercial activity, and capital, are subdued at the civically minded SFMOMA. The Fisher Galleries, which must predominantly (although not exclusively) house works on long-term loan from the eponymous family,[18] flow seamlessly into the museum's other galleries, including the very fine ones preserved from the Botta building. Snøhetta's ingenious stairwells have vanquished the special hell of riding escalators in an art museum, which conjures the feeling of being in a mall or an airport, commercial venues where moving people is the paramount concern. And only one small store has been added in the expansion, in the thrumming new lobby. All museums, but particularly ones as large as SFMOMA, are ecosystems, and these decisions impart a clear message about the museum's priorities: contemplation over consumption.

Delicious anecdotes dot SFMOMA's history. A 1940 Picasso show proved so popular that some 1,300 guests refused to leave on closing night, staging a sit-in that made the national papers.[19] Morley held the first solo museum show for Arshile Gorky, in 1941, as well as the first for Jackson Pollock, in 1945. Some seventy years later, Matthew Barney hung from a rope in the Botta atrium and made a drawing that still appears in its oculus. These achievements were realized with relatively modest means—in the staid War Memorial building ("cramped and outmoded," according to a 1995 report[20]) and then in the Botta, which had only 50,000 square feet of exhibition space, about a third of that available in the new structure.

Before the Botta opened, SFMOMA's collection was largely considered significant on a regional scale rather than an international one. But buildings can inspire donors to give, and its collection has grown. Timed with the expansion, the Campaign for Art brought in 3,000 new pieces: one hopes collectors will continue to step up. The new building is attuned to the needs of both historical and contemporary art, with galleries conceived to accommodate massive works but also ones that can be easily configured into intimate spaces. The light is superb. Emanating indirectly from a system of coves that hold LED lights, it is the sort of natural-looking light that even five years ago could not have been achieved. It ranks among the best light that I have ever seen in an art museum, up there with the Menil Collection in Houston and the Centre Pompidou in Paris.

A remarkable interplay takes place at SFMOMA between the inside and the outside, the natural and the artificial. The architects have found numerous ways of getting visitors to natural light, incorporating it in judicious but alluring ways. There are those large bay windows in the city galleries, but there are also the windows on the fifth floor of the Botta building, long closed for exhibition purposes, which Snøhetta was able to reopen, making a new room for sculptures. And there are terraces, including a long, thin one on the seventh floor, just a few steps from the galleries, that provide not only light but also some air. That balcony serves another special function: it allows you to grab that rippling façade, to feel its rough surface and its unexpected lightness, to get to know the material that makes such magic down on the street.

Building behemoths to accommodate outsized installations, many institutions participating in the recent museum boom experienced a curious amnesia about the role that architecture can play in elucidating artworks. Partially, this is the result of an overemphasis in curatorial thinking about the autonomy of modernist artworks and the hegemony of the white cube as the default mode of exhibition design, which casts aside some of the great milestones of twentieth-century art: the Rothko Chapel in Houston, arrayed with paintings the artist made in the mid-1960s; *The Dance,* created by Matisse from 1932 to 1933 for a wall in Dr. Alfred C. Barnes's gallery in Merion, Pennsylvania; and the *Water Lilies*, which Monet painted with an ovular room configuration specifically in mind, displayed at the Musée de l'Orangerie in Paris since 1927. At SFMOMA there is a wonderful response to this forgetting. An octagonal room is tucked at one end of the fourth-floor Fisher Galleries, a bit beyond the tour-de-force Ellsworth Kelly spaces. The room contains an array of seven pieces by Agnes Martin, a lone circular sofa at its center. It feels like a devotional space. This secret place of repose is the sort of room that comes to define a museum, that makes a space a place. It is a room that people will tell each other about, that visitors will go hunting for and will return to again and again. As with the other custom-built exhibition spaces, our heart aches for the visitor who misses it.

How do you help the entire museum ecosystem work? How do you make it hum? These are concerns that extend far beyond gallery design. Answers arrive on the top three floors of the museum, in the administrative offices, which offer breathtaking vistas, great helpings of natural light, and even outdoor balconies for employees. Curators are not known for having particularly pleasant office environs, and so these rooms delineate an ethos for SFMOMA, a belief that aesthetics really do have spillover effects, that they can improve the quality of what is happening on the floors below.

Other specialized spaces have also been reimagined, and in some cases new ones have been added. The theater, now accessible through a dedicated entrance for after-hour events, is a thing of beauty, framed with gracefully curving dividers by the San Francisco firm EHDD. A bare-bones coffee shop is situated on the third floor, at a nexus point, just off the Alexander Calder Gallery, the capacious photography galleries, and the stairwell leading up to the first city gallery. That is a bold play, risking congestion, but it seems to be functioning as an action-packed gathering point, a ski chalet right at the base of the mountain.

On the fourth floor is a space with soaring ceilings dubbed the White Box, conceived as a place for all manner of activities—performances or lectures or events. It is just a few steps from the galleries, underscoring the sensible position that disciplines should be experienced in tandem, that artworks cannot be shunted off into separate compartments for separate audiences.

On the last publicly accessible floor, number seven, the terrace looks in on a double-height conservation lab, blurring the boundary between public and private space. The lab also has room for artists to be in residence, consulting on work and making new pieces, which engenders another blurring, this time between conservation and curatorial activities. All of this suggests a museum that is as comfortable producing art as it is preserving it—a freezer and an oven, both state of the art.

This is an electrifying moment for art museums, and an anxious one. As the digital encroaches on every aspect of life, with screens replacing objects and the manipulation of information replacing the handling of actual things, coming face to face with the actual raw material of culture is going to become both more important and more charged. This will occur in museums, which are redoubts of the real. The essential question they must ask themselves now is how to best facilitate these experiences, to enrich them in discerning ways.

Marioni presents one model: by playing the consummate host, offering up a venue for shared sociality and for individual pleasure—a place for being alone together. The artist Robert Barry has proposed what one might think of as the East Coast-serious version of Marioni's work, simply writing on a wall in *Marcuse Piece* (1970): "A place to which we can come and for a while 'be free to think about what we are going to do.'" That is what museums can accomplish at their very best: placing the visitor in a state of absolute freedom and charging time with a rich sense of possibility.

That is the same feeling that a good, dense urban environment can impart as one strolls through its neighborhoods. In its sheer scale, its layers of offerings, one might think of SFMOMA as a city unto itself, as my colleague Roberta Smith has suggested.[21] Indeed, its size stuns—but it does not overwhelm. Its gullies and passageways provide an environment for unhurried exploration. Tourists will no doubt aim to see it all, but locals can now approach SFMOMA in an unusual way, more as a library than a museum—a place to return to repeatedly, to happen upon new things, while always aware that old favorites are there.

Walter Benjamin defended the importance of having a library that exceeds one's grasp, writing about a "philistine" who visited Anatole France and admired his collection, leading to this exchange: "'And you have read all these books, Monsieur France?' 'Not one-tenth of them. I don't suppose you use your Sevres china every day?'"[22] Not one-tenth of them. SFMOMA now has 33,000 works in its collection, and a building that allows visitors revel in that vastness. And intriguingly, now that its collection is allowed to stretch out, the museum is, in a sense, returning to its roots in the packed *Wunderkammern* of the Renaissance—repositories for every kind of wild treasure, places for disparate encounters, pedagogical, erotic, and aesthetic.

Up on the seventh floor, near a window that looks out onto the city, is Charles Ray's milled steel sculpture *Sleeping Woman* (2012). She appears to be homeless, resting on a bench. At a glance, she seems perfectly carved, but then you look closely: her precise details go mysteriously in and out of focus. It "aspires to be a monument, but one in our own realm rather than beyond it," SFMOMA's senior curator of painting and sculpture, Gary Garrels, writes of the piece.[23] Shimmering and reflective, she seems to be always changing, on the verge of evanescing at any moment. This is a condition not unlike the façade of the Snøhetta building: glowing lilac in the afternoon, but only fleetingly, continually on the verge of becoming something else.

That, of course, is true of us all, and one of art's powers has always been to help make sense of that flux, all the while posing other queries: How do we navigate space? How do we find ourselves within it? These are difficult questions. As Ray once told me, "When you talk you're always moving or shaking, or your hands are going… that vibration makes you bigger as one experiences you."[24] Even when we think we are present, paying attention to what we are doing and who we are, we escape ourselves.

And so we stroll the stairs along the city galleries, taking in views of San Francisco and trying to anticipate what will come next, readying ourselves for it. The building works on us. It revitalizes us and gently encourages us to see better, to think more deeply. Ray also has said, "The act of making the sculpture and the sculpture itself create a sort of meaning machine that, when the work is good, is hard, if not impossible, to turn off."[25] That is true of architecture, too.

Art Is for Living

What was a museum? In antiquity, it was a collection of texts and artworks, a temple of the Muses. The *Musaeum* at Alexandria, where scholars and artists lived in communal quarters, was both a library and a generator of knowledge, science, culture, and poetry. Later, the collections themselves became the focus as wealthy patrons amassed oddities and treasures in special rooms, cabinets of curiosities, within their homes. Many fine arts museums have preserved this tradition by displaying collections, now publicly accessible but protected within stately monumental repositories.

A journey through a museum today can be a serious commitment. Spaces are stripped bare and white walls have become the norm in modern art galleries. As useful as this may appear to be, such spaces can also seem austere and unfriendly. The white cube is a kind of neutral space, but it is also very much a statement about framing art as an exalted object. Art galleries are often very different from the messy, daylit studio environments where art is made. How could the contemporary gallery formula be reimagined to create a more energizing, yet still serene, space for art?

A museum that only offers one kind of experience, whatever that may be, will bring on fatigue much more quickly than one that allows people to move fast or slow, to stop and sit, to bypass areas or change their route. Likewise, a building that is dominated by variation is confusing. Either way, the experience of art is compromised. So finding balance is important. This balance helps maintain intimacy in both life and art.

Artworks are often experienced surrounded by strangers, sometimes even in crowds. Is it possible to preserve an individual experience with art? Even when facing a great work of art with friends, there may still be a desire for contemplation, to experience the work alone. Architecture can provide moments of devotional space, accessing the intimate scale of a small gallery hidden within a larger institution.

At the end of the day, after the crowds have left and the lights are dimmed, a museum continues to live. Its floors are readied for the next day, its curators work into the night arranging ideas for the future, its administration wrangles with upcoming challenges, and the security staff settle in for a long night of looking at art in a different way than most people ever will.

Following the conventions of its time, the Botta building fit SFMOMA's collection into a series of discrete "white cube" spaces, intimate in scale and appropriate for viewing the museum's art, but hermetically sealed off from the outside world.

SFMOMA thoughtfully expanded its collection of modern and contemporary art over time. It is now recognized internationally for its complexity and richness. They have also developed rich educational and social programs to support the museum's goal of relevance in the world around it. Similarly, the Fisher family, founders of The Gap, lovingly assembled their own rich collection, living among their favorite works. Their collection is very personal. They are known to have taken their favorite Gerhard Richter with them on vacation, wrapped in towels in the back of the station wagon.

When SFMOMA and the Fishers decided to merge their collections, both agreed that the museum should not feel divided. Works from the Fisher Family Collection would be exhibited as a group but integrated into the expanded building in such a way that no threshold would mark a Fisher "wing" or SFMOMA gallery.

Snøhetta, SFMOMA, and the Fishers worked together to establish the gallery design criteria. A series of workshops brought multiple worlds of thinking together.

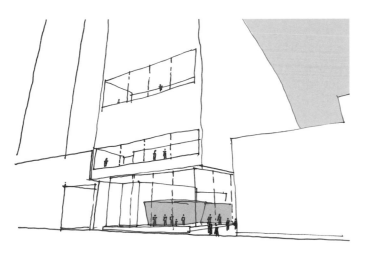

The expansion brings art to the street. Along what was once a sleepy stretch of Howard Street, the ground-level gallery activates a new civic space that supports casual, daily interaction with art.

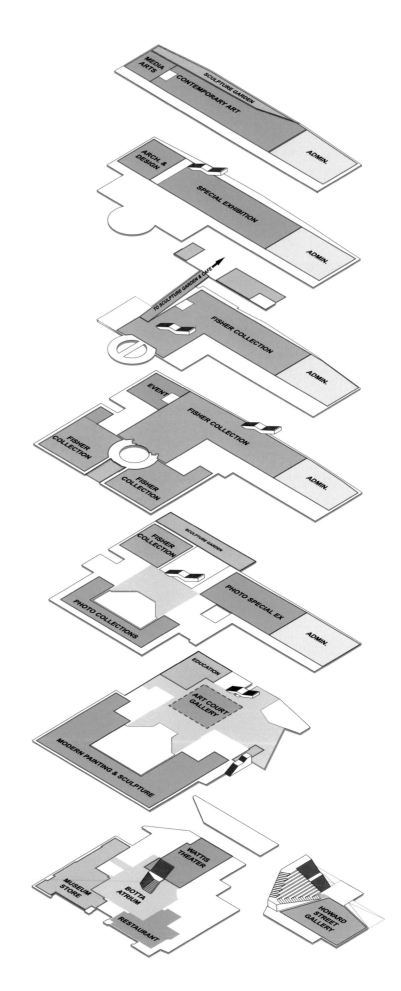

An early version of the gallery map shows a slightly different arrangement of public galleries and administrative offices.

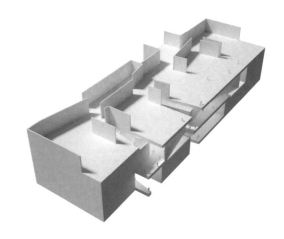

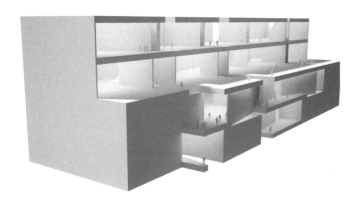

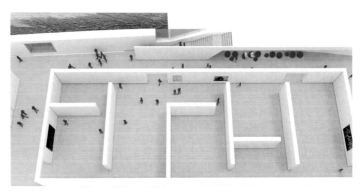

To create a variety of pace and atmosphere, we located a series of "core gallery" spaces in the center of the new footprint. These spaces are carefully designed to be calm and focused, containing exhibition areas with a few select points where visitors can rest or view interstitial spaces. These "core galleries" are in the same area on every floor. They may employ a family of solutions related to different parts of the collection, but they provide a recognizable anchor for visitors.

At each end of the building plan, along Minna and Howard Streets, there are destination galleries which are new ingredients to the gallery experience. These galleries break with the rigor of the core galleries and have more defined individual identities.

The City Gallery and elevator lobby connect the galleries. These social spaces wrap around the main galleries, providing places to pause while protecting the quieter core.

Long structural spans ensure that temporary walls can be arranged according to the needs of the art or left out altogether. Given their diverse character, the galleries come together as a collection of neighborhoods. The scale is intimate but also open, allowing visitors to focus on one exhibit or experience many during a single visit.

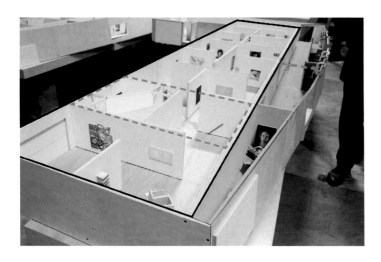

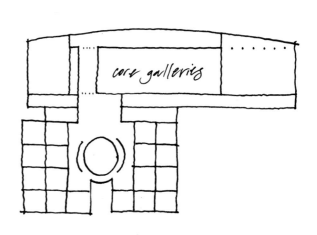

core galleries

Subtle engagement of the senses within the galleries creates an intimate and memorable experience within the complex surroundings.

Light quality is the most elusive yet most critical element in any gallery. We studied various possibilities in model form, building many different types of ceiling conditions and light effects. Technical infrastructure is hidden from view so that the visitor's gaze is allowed to focus on the exhibitions.

Floating maple flooring and acoustically tuned ceilings soften footfalls and produce ideal conditions for comfortable conversation.

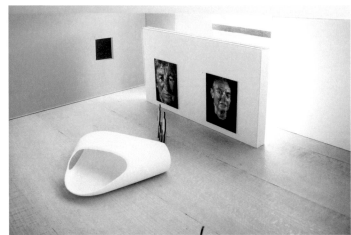

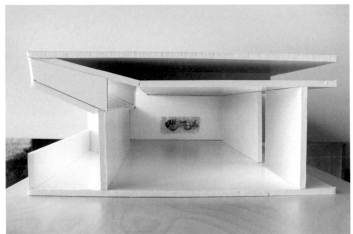

Technical models explored the performance of different ceiling cove forms to determine the design most optimal for viewing art. We found that linear LED fixtures, tucked inside coves with a highly refined profile, can create a soft ambient light evocative of natural daylight.

A second system of LED track lights provides a layer of focused object lighting, used to highlight wall and floor pieces. These studies illustrate the asymmetrical coves: light enters the gallery space from the same direction as the natural light entering through the City Gallery windows nearby.

The lighting supports concentration and quiet as well as vibrancy and dynamism.

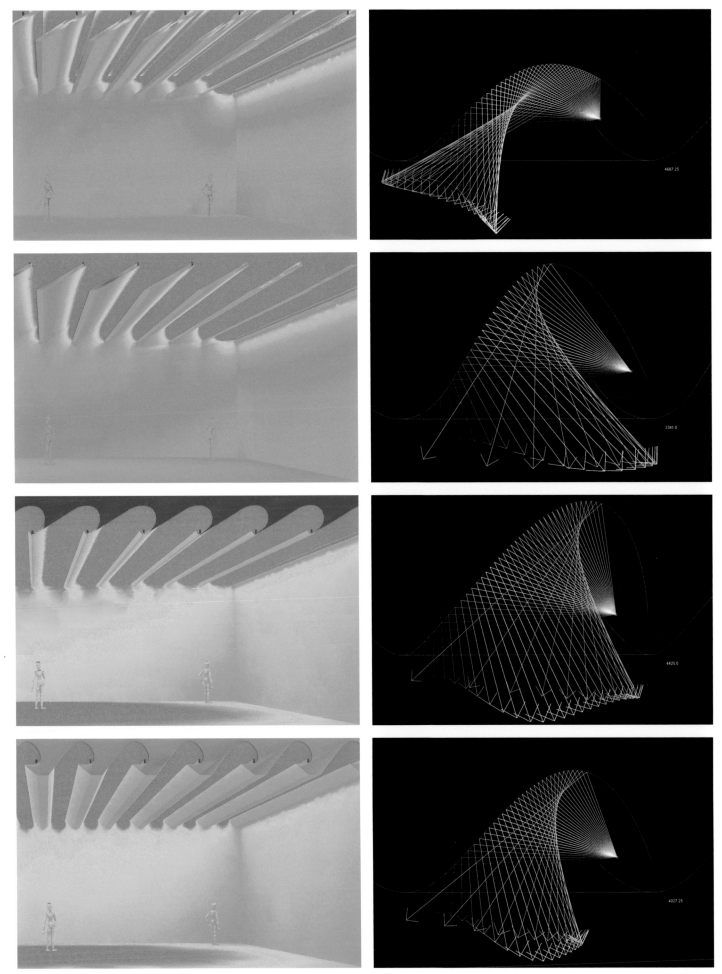

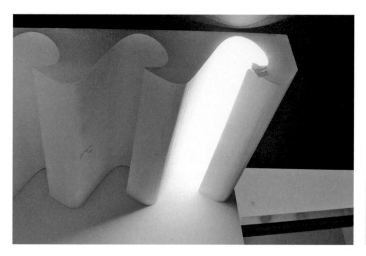

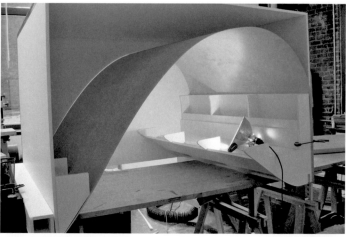

The iterative process of testing physical form and construction methods involved many different hands, minds, and materials. The review of a full-scale mock-up before construction began confirmed the ultimate performance and aesthetic goals of the project.

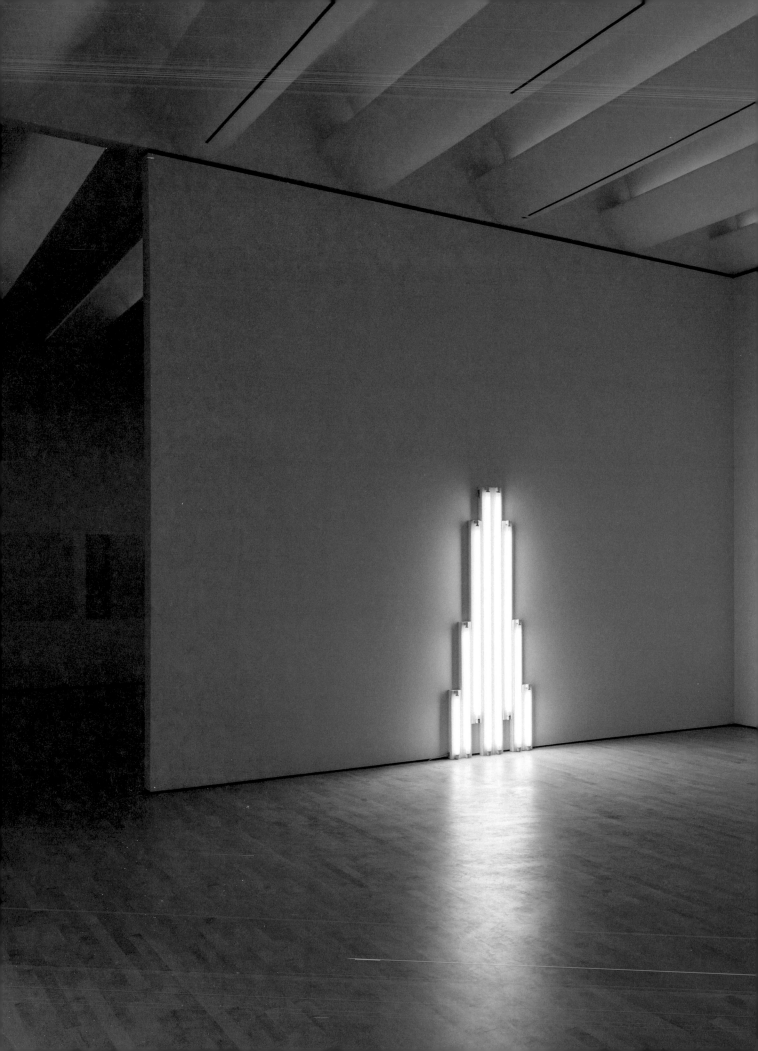

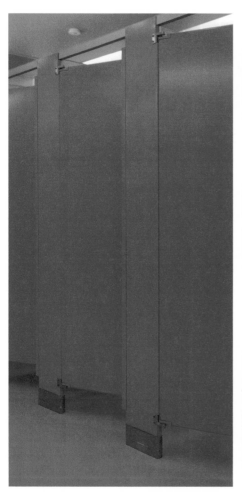

Notes from "Coming into Sight"

1 "Tom Marioni: The Act of Drinking Beer," video published by the Smart Museum of Art, Chicago, March 5, 2012, https://vimeo.com/37981379. SFMOMA acquired a version of the work in 1999.

2 Like so many of Stein's witticisms, no definitive source for this line has been found, but it is widely attributed to her, as in James E. B. Breslin, *Mark Rothko: A Biography* (Chicago: University of Chicago Press, 1993), 137.

3 Theodor W. Adorno, "Valéry Proust Museum" (1953), in *On the Museum's Ruins*, ed. Douglas Crimp and Louise Lawler (Cambridge, MA: MIT Press, 1993), 44.

4 Craig Dykers, in conversation with the author, New York, July 21, 2016. See also Dan Howarth, "'We Could Never Recreate Mario Botta's SFMOMA' Says Extension Architect Craig Dykers of Snøhetta," *Dezeen*, May 2, 2016, http://www.dezeen.com/2016/05/02/san-francisco-museum-of-modern-art-sfmoma-extension-interview-snohetta-craig-dykers-ruth-berson-mario-botta/.

5 I love Roberta Smith's observation that the building resembles an Achrome by Piero Manzoni, as she says in "SFMOMA's Expansion Sets a New Standard for Museums," *New York Times*, May 13, 2016, http://www.nytimes.com/2016/05/14/arts/design/review-san-francisco-museum-of-modern-art-expansion.html.

6 Pae White's large, bewitching tapestry *Smoke Knows* (2009), in which swirling white clouds of smoke appear against a black backdrop, also feels like a fruitful comparison. SFMOMA acquired the work in 2010.

7 The line provided the title for Lawrence Weschler's magnificent Irwin biography, *Seeing Is Forgetting the Name of the Thing One Sees* (Berkeley: University of California Press, 1982), 203.

8 SFMOMA owns a large installation of these works, *Atrabiliarios* (1992–2003), which it acquired in 2004.

9 Dykers, in conversation with the author.

10 Google Map of "local inspiration," provided to the author by architect Lara Kaufman of Snøhetta.

11 Dykers, in conversation with the author.

12 This reading is indebted to Christopher Butler's description of the *flâneur* in his *Early Modernism: Literature, Music, and Painting in Europe, 1900–1916* (Oxford: Oxford University Press, 1994), 133.

13 Hal Foster, *The Art-Architectural Complex* (New York: Verso, 2011), xii.

14 Ibid., xi–xii.

15 Robert Morris, *Have I Reasons: Work and Writings, 1993–2007* (Durham, NC: Duke University Press, 2008), 132.

16 Ibid., 134.

17 The corporate baroque, it should be noted, is very far from dead, as evidenced by Gehry's Fondation Louis Vuitton in Paris (2014).

18 Seventy-five percent of the work on view in these galleries must come from the Fisher Collection, and every ten years a show devoted to that work must be presented there.

19 The United Press reported this story, which appeared in various papers throughout the United States, including the *St. Petersburg Times*, August 16, 1940, under the headline, "Art Visitors Stage Sit-Down." It reads in full, "This city believes it can claim the honor of having staged the first art sit-down strike in history. When the 10 o'clock closing hour at the San Francisco Museum of Arts, where an extensive collection of Picasso's paintings were being shown, arrived for the last day of the display, 1,300 visitors sat down and refused to leave till they had their fill."

20 Joan Smith, "S.F. Meets Its New MOMA," *San Francisco Chronicle*, January 1, 1995, http://www.sfgate.com/bayarea/article/S-F-meets-its-new-MOMA-3160923.php.

21 Roberta Smith, "SFMOMA's Expansion." She writes, "[SFMOMA] feels like a small city, which is a singular achievement in terms of both architecture and collection building."

22 Walter Benjamin, *Illuminations*, trans. Harry Zohn (New York: Schocken Books, 1968), 62.

23 Gary Garrels, "Gary Garrels on *Sleeping Woman*," in *San Francisco Museum of Modern Art 360°: Views on the Collection*, ed. Judy Bloch and Suzanne Stein (San Francisco: SFMOMA, 2016), 346.

24 Andrew Russeth, "Shoeless Ray," *New York Observer*, November 19, 2012, http://observer.com/2012/11/charles-ray-at-matthew-marks-gallery-2012/.

25 Charles Ray, quoted in Umberta Genta, "Charles Ray: Using Time," *Flash Art*, January/February 2013, 52.

About Snøhetta

Snøhetta values human interaction. All of our work strives to enhance our sense of place, identity, and relationship to others and the physical spaces we inhabit, whether natural or human-made. Art museums, reindeer observatories, urban places, and dollhouses receive the same care and attention to purpose.

For over twenty-five years, we have been working internationally on a number of important educational, civic, and cultural projects. Snøhetta formed as a company after a loosely knit group won the international design competition for the new library of Alexandria, Egypt, in 1989. This was later followed by the commission for the Norwegian National Opera and Ballet in Oslo and the National September 11 Memorial Museum Pavilion at the World Trade Center in New York City, along with the expansion of the San Francisco Museum of Modern Art and the King Abdulaziz Center for World Culture in Dhahran, Saudi Arabia. Recently completed works include the redesign of the public space in Times Square, the Lascaux IV Caves Museum in Montignac, France, and a series of net-zero energy projects as part of the Powerhouse Alliance. Snøhetta is currently designing the Willamette Falls Riverwalk in Oregon City, Oregon, The French Laundry Kitchen Expansion and Garden Renovation in Yountville, California, and many others.

Among its many recognitions, Snøhetta received the World Architecture Award for the Bibliotheca Alexandrina and the Norwegian National Opera and Ballet, and the Aga Khan Award for Architecture for the Bibliotheca Alexandrina. Since its completion in 2008, the Norwegian National Opera and Ballet has also garnered the Mies van der Rohe European Union Prize for Contemporary Architecture and the EDRA (Environmental Design Research Association) Great Places Award, as well as the European Prize for Urban Public Space, the International Architecture Award, and the Global Award for Sustainable Architecture. In 2016, Snøhetta was named the *Wall Street Journal*'s Architecture Innovator of the Year. The SFMOMA expansion was the recipient of *The Architect's Newspaper*'s 2016 Building of the Year › West Design Award, as well as the 2016 WIN Museum Interior Award.

Since its inception, the firm has maintained its transdisciplinary approach. Snøhetta operates as a collaborative studio where architects, landscape architects, interior designers, and brand designers sit side by side in open-plan spaces.

Contributors

Rebecca Solnit
Writer, historian, and activist Rebecca Solnit is the author of eighteen or so
books on feminism, western and indigenous history, popular power, social
change and insurrection, wandering and walking, hope and disaster, including
a trilogy of atlases and the books *Men Explain Things to Me; The Faraway
Nearby; A Paradise Built in Hell: The Extraordinary Communities that Arise in
Disaster; A Field Guide to Getting Lost; Wanderlust: A History of Walking;*
and *River of Shadows: Eadweard Muybridge and the Technological Wild West*
(for which she received a Guggenheim award, the National Book Critics Circle
Award in criticism, and the Lannan Literary Award). The Muybridge book,
like her first book, first atlas, and her report in 2000 from the dot-com boom,
Hollow City: The Siege of San Francisco and the Crisis of American Urbanism,
focuses on San Francisco, where she has lived since she was eighteen.
A product of the California public education system from kindergarten to
graduate school, she is a columnist at *Harper's*.

Justin Davidson
Justin Davidson is the architecture and classical music critic at *New York*
magazine, where he writes about a broad range of urban, civic, and design
issues. He grew up in Rome, graduated from Harvard, and later earned
a doctoral degree in music composition at Columbia University. As a classical
music and cultural critic at *Newsday,* he won a Pulitzer Prize for criticism in
2002. He is the author of *Magnetic City: A Walking Companion to New York*
(Random House, 2017).

Andrew Russeth
Andrew Russeth is an art critic based in New York. Co-executive editor of
ARTnews, he previously co-founded and edited GalleristNY, the *New York
Observer*'s website about the New York art world. His writing has appeared in
W, New York, Modern Painters, Art+Auction, Bijutsu Techo, and the *New Yorker*'s
website, as well as catalogues for exhibitions at the Whitney Museum of
American Art, the Studio Museum in Harlem, and other museums and galleries.
16 Miles of String, his blog about contemporary art and art history in New York,
has been supported by the Creative Capital | Warhol Foundation Arts Writers
Grant Program.

Nancy Eklund Later
Trained as an architectural historian, Nancy Eklund Later works as a freelance
editor specializing in books on architecture, design, and the built environment. She has assisted authors and publishers in the development of well
over one hundred books. She lives with her husband and daughter in
New York City.

Acknowledgments

Many thousands of people are necessary to build a work of architecture such as the SFMOMA, including benefactors, administration teams, curators, designers, engineers, managers, city planners, city council members, lawyers, agents, manufacturers, and builders. Such numbers make it challenging to thank everyone specifically. However, we can say that all are greatly appreciated and the skill and energy provided by this village inspired us all at Snøhetta. Among these we cannot forget the positive energy given us by those who work the floors at SFMOMA, the day-to-day staff who always welcomed us with a smile and kind words.

We would like to point out a few people who were more specifically impactful. Neal Benezra and the SFMOMA curatorial team focused our awareness of how art and people interact. Ruth Berson could always be trusted to nurture stability in even the roughest waters. Bob Fisher showed us the power of generosity and warmth. Doris Fisher and her family provided us with the power of a meaningful life and caring family. Chuck and Helen Schwab cast sensitivity and a discerning eye upon a challenging process. Dennis Wong protected the project when the tough questions had to be asked. Mimi Haas pushed our imagination with her tireless and profound energy. The SFMOMA Board inspired the design through their devotion and patience. David Meckel's keen sensibilities helped guide our selection as the architect, it is hard to thank him enough. Stanley Saitowitz provided us with early advice and guidance on our architectural approach. Our project managers, Terry Reagan and Don Young, alongside Duncan Ballash and the EHDD team, were always great partners and helped the project mature to what you experience today. Finally, we would like to thank the Fang family, who operate Fang Restaurant next door... they put up with the construction and cooked us so many amazing meals, each one a special memory.

Project Team

Snøhetta: Design Architect & Architect of Record,
Landscape Architect, and Interior Designer

Snøhetta Design Team:
Nick Anderson
Behrang Behin
Samuel Brissette
Chad Carpenter
Michael Cotton
Aaron Dorf
Craig Dykers
Simon Ewings
Aroussiak Gabrielian
Alan Gordon
Kyle Johnson
Lara Kaufman
Nick Koster
Marianne Lau
Jon McNeal
Mario Mohan
Elaine Molinar
Neda Mostafavi
Maura Rockcastle
Anne-Rachel Schiffmann
Kjetil Trædal Thorsen
Carrie Tsang
Giancarlo Valle

Associate Architect, EHDD:
Duncan Ballash
Lotte Kaefer
Rebecca Sharkey
Kelly Ishida Sloan

Engineers & Consultants:
Structural: Magnusson Klemencic Associates
Mechanical & Plumbing: Taylor Engineering
Electrical: The Engineering Enterprise
Civil: KPFF
Lighting (galleries, public spaces): Arup
Lighting (administrative areas): The Engineering Enterprise
Acoustics & AV: Arup
Façade: Arup
Façade Design Assist Contractor: Enclos, Kreysler & Associates
Telcom: TEECOM
Security: Turk Technologies
Conservation Lab & Art Storage: Samuel Anderson Architects
Living Wall: Habitat Horticulture / Hyphae Design Lab
Sustainability: Atelier Ten
LEED: EHDD
Façade Maintenance: CS Caulkins
Fire Life Safety & Code: The Fire Consultants
Graphics & Signage: SOM Graphics
Waterproofing: McGinnis Chen Associates
Hardware: Allegion

General Contractor:
Webcor Builders

Image Credits

Unless otherwise stated, all drawings, model views, photographs of projects designed by Snøhetta, and photographs of San Francisco appear courtesy of Snøhetta. The following credits apply to all images for which separate acknowledgment is due.

22 left: Cartography Associates, Sanborn-Perris Map Company, Limited, 1905
22 top right three photos: San Francisco History Center, San Francisco Public Library
22 bottom right: Turner Construction, San Francisco History Center, San Francisco Public Library
23 top left: Wayne Thiebaud, *Valley Streets,* © Wayne Thiebaud / Licensed by VAGA, New York
23 top right: Janet Delaney, *Flag Makers, Natoma at Third Street,* from the series *South of Market, 1978–1986,* © Janet Delaney
23 bottom right: Rigo 23, Study for *Looking at 1998 San Francisco from the Top of 1925,* © Rigo 23
23 bottom left: Robert Bechtle, *Sunset Tercel,* © Robert Bechtle, Courtesy Anglim Gilbert Gallery
24 top left, 25 top left: Courtesy SFMOMA Archives
24 top middle: Chris Carlsson
24 top right: Michael Layefsky
25 top right: SFMOMA [aerial photo], May 31 2007. Google Earth. Map Data © 2007 Google
25 bottom left, 209 bottom left: Richard Barnes, Courtesy SFMOMA
25 bottom right: William Mercer McLeod
41, 42, 47, 138, 144, 152, 154, 156, 158, 159, 161, 166, 170, 174, 238, 241, 248 bottom, 256, 262: © Jeff Goldberg / Esto
59: Photo: Snøhetta, Artwork: Alexander Calder, *Big Crinkly,* © 2017 Calder Foundation, New York / Artists Rights Society (ARS), New York
61, 163, 164, 165, 179, 234, 242, 246, 254, 257: Michael Grimm
62: Drew Altizer
83, 89, 99, 100 bottom, 134, 142, 209 bottom right, 223, 274: Henrik Kam
116 top right: Fred Lyon, *North Beach Houses, Montgomery Street, 1949,* © Fred Lyon / Courtesy Peter Fetterman Gallery
117 bottom right: Photo: Snøhetta, Artwork: Isamu Noguchi, *The Roar,* 1966, © 2017 The Isamu Noguchi Foundation and Garden Museum, NY / Artists Rights Society (ARS), New York
118 right: Fred Lyon, *Night Scene on Nob Hill,* © Fred Lyon / Courtesy Peter Fetterman Gallery
144: Photo: © Jeff Goldberg / Esto, Artwork: Alexander Calder, *Maquette for Trois disques* formerly *Man,* © 2017 Calder Foundation, New York / Artists Rights Society (ARS), New York

208 top left: O. Von Corven, *The Great Library of Alexandria*
208 top right: David Teniers the Younger, *Archduke Leopold Wilhelm in his Gallery,* 1951, Courtesy of Museo Nacional del Prado
208 bottom right: Pablo Picasso, *Guernica,* 1937. Installation view, San Francisco Museum of Modern Art, 1939
208 bottom left: Installation view of the 77th Annual Painting and Sculpture Exhibition of the San Francisco Art Association, 1958, Courtesy SFMOMA
209 top middle: Walter Landor, *Space for Living: An Exhibition of Planning and Architecture,* 1940; exhibition poster from *Dispatches from the Archives* exhibition at SFMOMA, Courtesy SFMOMA Archives
209 top right: Tapio Wirkkala, Design in Scandinavia, 1957; poster from *Dispatches from the Archives* exhibition at SFMOMA; Courtesy SFMOMA Archives
219 left four images: Arup
233: Photo: Snøhetta, Artwork: George Segal, *Chance Meeting,* 1989, cast 2004, © The George and Helen Segal Foundation / Licensed by VAGA, New York
234: Photo: Michael Grimm, Artwork: Alexander Calder, *Big Crinkly,* © 2017 Calder Foundation, New York / Artists Rights Society (ARS), New York
252: Photo: Snøhetta, Artwork: Dan Flavin, *"Monument" for V. Tatlin,* © 2017 Stephen Flavin / Artists Rights Society (ARS), New York